Early Nineteenth-Century
American Diary Literature

Twayne's United States Authors Series

David J. Nordloh, Editor

Indiana University

TUSAS 495

Manuscript page from the journal of Ralph Waldo Emerson
By permission of the Ralph Waldo Emerson Memorial Association and the Houghton Library

Early Nineteenth-Century American Diary Literature

By Steven E. Kagle

Illinois State University

Twayne Publishers • *Boston*

Early Nineteenth-Century
American Diary Literature

Steven E. Kagle

Copyright © 1986 by G. K. Hall & Company
All Rights Reserved
Published by Twayne Publishers
A Division of G. K. Hall & Company
70 Lincoln Street
Boston, Massachusetts 02111

Copyediting supervised by Lewis DeSimone
Book Production by Lyda E. Kuth
Book Design by Barbara Anderson

Typeset in 11 pt. Garamond
by Compset, Inc. of Beverly, Massachusetts

Printed on permanent/durable acid-free paper
and bound in the United States of America.

Library of Congress Cataloging in Publication Data

Kagle, Steven E.
    Early nineteenth-century American diary literature.

    (Twayne's United States authors series ; TUSAS 495)
    Bibliography: p. 156
    Includes index.
    1. American diaries—History and criticism. 2.
American prose literature—19th century—History and criticism.
3. United States—History—1783–1865—Biography. I. Title.   II. Series.
PS409.K33   1986   818'.203 [B]   85-17626
ISBN 0-8057-7454-8

For my parents,
Dr. Estelle P. Kagle
and
Dr. Louis Kagle

Contents

About the Author

Steven E. Kagle is professor of English at Illinois State University, where he teaches colonial and nineteenth-century American literature, creative writing, and science fiction literature. He received an A.B. degree in English from Cornell University and holds an M.A. in English and a Ph.D. in American culture from the University of Michigan.

In addition to this volume Professor Kagle is the author of *American Diary Literature 1607–1800*. He is the editor of three books: *The Diary of Josiah Atkins* (New York Times and Arno Press, 1975), *Plymouth* (by Carol Gesner, published by *Exploration,* 1976), and *America: Exploration and Travel* (Popular Press of Bowling Green University, 1979). In addition he is the author of a number of shorter works; among these are several dealing with diary literature, including "Diary of John Adams and the Motive of Achievement" *(Hartford Studies in Literature,* 1971), "Diary as Art: A New Assessment" *(Genre,* 1973), and entries in *American Writers before 1800* (Greenwood Press, 1983) and *Dictionary of Literary Biography: American Literature of the Revolution and Early National Period* (Gale Research, 1985). For ten years he served as editor of *Exploration,* a scholarly journal on the literature of travel and exploration. Professor Kagle is currently working on a study of the diary literature written in America during the last half of the nineteenth century as well as on a novel.

Preface

In writing this book, I have attempted to continue the work, which I began in my earlier volume for this series, *American Diary Literature 1607–1800*, of establishing the canon of American diaries with intrinsic literary merit. No single scholar can or should make such a determination alone, but the work has to begin somewhere. It is my hope that this work will open this rich body of literature to future scholarship.

In my earlier book I was able to treat only twenty-seven diaries; however, I felt confident that I had covered most of the important works as well as a number of the more interesting minor diaries. In this work, covering only half of one century, I have tried to deal with about the same number and even then I have had to deal with some only briefly and omit entirely many diaries worthy of study. Not only did the number of American diaries increase with the growing population, but the size of the diaries also increased substantially. John Adams's diary was one of the longest colonial diaries; and yet it is small compared to that of his son, John Quincy Adams. Alcott, Emerson, and Hone each wrote diaries running into the millions of words, dwarfing not only any single colonial diary but, when taken together, exceeding the size of all the diaries covered in my earlier work.

Since my primary consideration in choosing works for this volume has been to select those works with intrinsic literary value, I have had to exclude many diaries that contained valuable insights and information but that had a lesser thematic coherence or stylistic skill. These works deserve to be studied, but I have not sought or pretended to do so here. I have given some preference to works that help to demonstrate important subgeneric categories; but, given the pressures of space, I could not even begin to represent every type of diarist, no less provide representative numbers of diaries from each class of diarist. I have also had to omit or deal only in passing with diaries written by foreigners in America, diaries written in languages other than English, and diaries existing only or primarily in a heavily altered form.

Another objective in writing this book was to offer a coherent interpretation of the most important diaries. While, especially for those of extreme length, I could hardly touch on every subject that deserves treatment, I have sought to provide an overview of each diary rather than a specialized treatment of a particular portion. In my examination of many of these diaries I have written the first studies of the works as literature; in some cases I have offered the first studies of the works from any perspective. However, I have neither sought nor hoped to have the last word. In "The American Scholar" Emerson wrote that no book should be seen as the final word on a subject because the "right use" of any book is "to inspire." My greatest wish for this work is that it may make this vast and varied body of literature sufficiently manageable that others will find it easier to apply their talents in studying it.

Steven E. Kagle

Illinois State University

Acknowledgments

I am indebted to the following institutions and their staffs for permission and assistance in using their libraries and other facilities: The American Antiquarian Society, the American Philosophical Society, the Boston Public Library, Columbia University, the Detroit Art Institute, the Eastham Public Library, Harvard University, Haverford College (especially the staff of the Quaker Collection), Illinois State University, the J. Pierpont Morgan Library, the Library of Congress, the Newberry Library, the New Jersey Historical Society, the New York Historical Society, the New York Public Library, the Pennsylvania Historical Society, the University of Illinois, the University of Wisconsin at Madison, and Yale University.

I am grateful to the following individuals and institutions for permission to quote from works bearing their copyright: Adams Manuscript Trust for the microfilm edition of *The Adams Papers* (1954); Alfred A. Knopf Inc. for *Journal of a Residence on a Georgia Plantation in 1838–1839* (1961); Dover Publications Inc. for *Audubon in his Journals* (1960); G. K. Hall & Co. for *The Complete Works of Washington Irving: Journals and Notebooks* (1969–81); Harvard University Press for *The Journals and Miscellaneous Notebooks of Ralph Waldo Emerson* (1960–82); Haskell House Publishers Ltd. for *The Journals of Washington Irving* (1970); Kraus Thompson Ltd. for *The Diary of Philip Hone 1828–1851* (1969); Little, Brown & Co. for *The Journals of Bronson Alcott* (1938); University of Illinois Press for *The Expeditions of John Charles Frémont* (1970); University of Oklahoma Press for *The 1826 Journal of John James Audubon* (1967), *The Journals and Letters of Zebulon Montgomery Pike: With Letters and Related Documents* (1966), *Exploring with Frémont: The Private Diaries of Charles Preuss, Cartographer for John C. Frémont on his First Second and Fourth Expeditions to the Far West* (1958), and *A Tour on the Prairies* (1956); and Yale University Press for *A Journey to Ohio in 1810* (1912).

I am also grateful to the following libraries for permission to quote from documents in their collections: the Houghton Library, Harvard University, for the manuscript of *The Journals of Amos Bronson Alcott* (1826–82); and the Quaker Collection, Haverford College Library, for the manuscript of *The Diary of Samuel Cole Davis* (1808–9).

I would also like to acknowledge the aid of my graduate assistants Andrew Bendelow and Enrica Brunelli and the support of Illinois State University for research grants that helped me to complete this work.

Finally, I would like to thank my wife, Jill, and my sons, Jonathan and Matthew, for their assistance and encouragement.

Chronology

1800   End of the presidency of John Adams.

1804   On orders from Thomas Jefferson, the Lewis and Clark expedition sets out to explore the Louisiana Purchase. They return in 1806.

1806   Zebulon Pike climbs Pike's Peak during his explorations in the Louisiana Territory.

1809   Samuel Cole Davis dies of "cancer."

1810   Margaret Van Horn Dwight (Bell) emigrates to Ohio.

1814   James Gallatin travels to Paris with his father, Albert Gallatin, who is going to join John Quincy Adams and others in negotiating the Treaty of Ghent ending the war of 1812.

1818   Henry Rowe Schoolcraft travels in the Ozarks.

1819   Botanist Thomas Nuttall travels through the Arkansas Territory.

1820   Washington Irving publishes *The Sketchbook of Geoffrey Crayon, Gent.*

1821   Theodore Dwight travels to Italy.

1823   James Fenimore Cooper begins his Leatherstocking novels with the publication of *Pioneers.*

1825   John Quincy Adams is elected president.

1826   John James Audubon begins the diary of a trip to Europe to arrange for the publication of his *Birds of America.*

1829   Thomas Cole leaves for Italy to paint and study, an event that prompts William Cullen Bryant to write his poem, "To Cole, the Painter, Departing for Europe."

1832   Francis Ann Kemble (Butler) begins her first diary about her experiences in America.

1835   Nathaniel Hawthorne begins his *American Notebooks.*

1836   Ralph Waldo Emerson publishes *Nature.*

1837   Financial Panic affects Philip Hone's fortune.

EARLY 19TH CENTURY AMERICAN DIARY LITERATURE

1839   Bronson Alcott closes his school after the uproar caused by his *Conversations on the Gospels.*

1842   Death of Emerson's son Waldo.

1843   John C. Frémont begins his second expedition, which will take him to Oregon and California.

1844   Bronson Alcott attempts to establish "Fruitlands" as a utopian community in Harvard, Massachusetts.

1845   Henry David Thoreau goes to Walden Pond, recording his experiences and thoughts in his journals.

1846   Francis Parkman explores the Oregon Trail.

1848   Mexican War ends.

1849   James K. Polk dies the same year he leaves the presidency.

Chapter One
The Diary in Nineteenth-Century America

Perhaps because the image of the frontier so dominates portraits of America's past in the media, few Americans are aware of how urbanized America's eastern cities had become in the first half of the nineteenth century. Most would be surprised to learn that by the time of the American Revolution the population of Philadelphia already rivaled that of any other English-speaking city save London itself. Still more surprising might be the density of the urban population. Instead of the charming merging of nature and society that can be seen in quaint small towns today, lithographs of major American cities in the first decade of the nineteenth century show row upon row of tall (three- to five-story) buildings stretching like walls along the streets. It was in or near these urbanized centers that Americans developed a sophisticated culture.

Even those cultural figures who worshiped nature were influenced by the life of the cities. A writer like Washington Irving or a painter like Thomas Cole might seek out and glorify the rustic charms of nature in the Catskill Mountains, but he also spent time in the urban world of New York City. Ralph Waldo Emerson might retreat to Concord, but Boston and Cambridge were only fifteen miles away. The reader of *Walden* may be lulled into imagining that Henry David Thoreau in 1845 had escaped from society, but his cabin at the pondside was only two miles away from the center of Concord. Partially as a result of the influence of the sophisticated culture of the urban centers, the diarists of the early nineteenth century were conscious of and affected by expectations of a public response.

The Colonial Tradition

The diary is one of the oldest literary forms written in America. The large number of surviving diaries kept by the early settlers is just one indication of how highly they and their descendants valued the practice.[1] One might expect that a large percentage of these diaries were begun in order that their authors might record their exploration of the New World, but this was not the case. The largest body of early diaries was kept by the Puritans, whose primary motive was a spiritual rather than a physical examination of their world. Diarists such as Michael Wigglesworth and David Brainerd tracked the internal development of their souls as an aid in their searches for salvation and the external events in their environment as a means to study God's messages revealed in His creation and providence. The records of a number of these Puritan diarists—most notably John Winthrop, Samuel Sewall, and Cotton Mather—are too complex to be classified simply as spiritual diaries, and yet they share many characteristics of that form.

While the Puritans were among the most prolific diarists, colonists of other faiths, especially the Quakers and Methodists, also valued the practice of diary keeping. One motive for diarists of both faiths was to follow the examples of their founders and leaders. Quakers such as John Woolman strove to emulate George Fox, founder of the Society of Friends, just as Francis Asbury followed the tradition of John Wesley, founder of Methodism. Many of these diarists hoped that their records might make their lives an example and an inspiration to others.

Special incidents prompted a number of colonial American diaries. Many diarists began their works in response to some event that promised to create or had already created disruptions in their normal lives. Among those events that most often prompted the writing of such *diaries of situation* in this period were travel, courtship, and war.

Just as the writers of spiritual journals used their works to strengthen their faiths, so American travel diarists in this period used their works to support their confidence in their social systems. Whether journeying for pleasure, health, or business, these travel diarists tried to record experiences that, when compared to those they had had at home, might confirm or redirect but rarely repudiate the values of their societies. Some diarists, such as Philip Vickers Fithian, emphasized the diversity among sections of the country. In the diary of his experiences while a tutor on a Virginia plantation Fithian spent a good deal of time criticizing slavery and its effects and so suggested the moral superiority of the society of his native New Jersey. Others, like Dr. Alexander Hamilton, might satirize the individuals and customs they encountered but still conclude that, while institutions might differ from section to section, there was "little difference in the manners and character of the people."[2]

Few events can so alter the course of a human life as love; and, therefore, numerous diaries are focused on periods of romance and courtship. These are as diverse as the experiences that inspire them. Those in the colonial period range from the light flirtations described in Sally Wister's diary to the tragic consequences in Ann Home Livingston's record.

There are numerous extant war diaries from the colonial period. Several were written during the French and Indian wars; however, many more—including those of the greatest literary value—were written during the American Revolution. Perhaps because of the demands of battle, few soldiers kept diaries of significant merit as literary works. The best diaries written by members of the army were those of individuals whose position usually kept them away from combat, for example, doctors like James Thacher. Other military diarists of note include Josiah Atkins, who spent a good portion of his service as a hospital orderly, and Charles Herbert, whose diary was written while its author was in a British prison. The Revolution affected all parts of American society, and a number of fine diaries of the war were kept by civilians, such as Margaret Morris, James Allen, and Samuel Rowland Fisher.

A few colonial diarists kept records that transcended the limits of some particular situation. Some of these *life diaries* began as *diaries of situation* but came to assume a more permanent and more general role in the lives of the diarists who produced them. Notable examples of life diaries kept in colonial America are those of John Winthrop, Samuel Sewall, William Byrd, Cotton Mather, and John Adams. The latter two diaries are worthy of special note because each is part of a series of diaries kept by members of the diarist's family stretching over several generations. These multigeneration diaries help to show that the habit of diary keeping was not totally private; rather, one individual's practice influenced others.

The Maturing Form

Literary historians have long asserted the magnitude and rapidity of the growth of American culture in the first half of the nineteenth century. Van Wyck Brooks wrote of a *Flowering of New England* culture during the second decade of the century culminating, during the early 1850s, in that period of amazing productivity that F. O. Matthiessen termed an *American Renaissance*. Because the diary was one of the first literary forms in America, some of the roots of this cultural growth can be observed in the metamorphosis of the American diary literature that took place in the first decade of the century.

This process is apparent in the volume of the diary literature written during the period covered in this book. The number of extant diaries of this period may, to a great extent, be explained by the increase in the population and loss of diaries over time, but there is no equally simple explanation for the great size of many of these diaries. While several colonial diaries such as those of Samuel Sewall, Cotton Mather, William Byrd, and John Adams are extensive and cover long periods in the lives of their authors, none of them come close to the volume of some major American diaries of the early nineteenth century. An incomplete edition of John Quincy Adams's diary runs twelve huge volumes; the most recent edition of Emerson's journals runs sixteen volumes; when completed, the Princeton edition of Thoreau's *Journals* should be almost as long; and if a complete edition of Bronson Alcott's diary is ever issued it will be far longer than any of these. The size of these journals is symptomatic of a general and relatively sudden shift toward longer diaries.

The length of such works is dramatic, but if length formed the single aspect of the change in American diary literature, it would be only a diverting curiosity. However, length is the most visible sign of a series of more complicated and significant changes. In general, the diaries of the early nineteenth century differ from their predecessors of the seventeenth and eighteenth centuries in the sophistication of their language and the variety of their concerns. While many of the best colonial diaries adhered to relatively simple forms with limited motives, the diaries of the early nineteenth century were more likely to mix elements of the diary of external incident with those of the introspective journal. Another important change is an increase in the diarists' consciousness of the diary's potential as a literary form.

To some extent these changes were responses to the absorption of elements of the Romantic movement into American culture. This movement with its emphasis on internal sources of truth is one reason a number of these diarists, justly famous for other writings and actions, pronounced the diary as offering the possibility for the highest achievement. However, Romanticism seems an insufficient explanation for these changes in the diary form. To really understand these changes one has to relate them to the diary form and to the Americans' new sense of national identity. The prolonged search for a clear national identity influenced an extension of the adolescent search for personal identity.

Public and Private Elements in American Diaries

One part of the change in American diary literature during this period involves audience. Relatively few colonial diaries were written with the intention of opening them to public scrutiny, but many of the diarists in early nineteenth-century America intended to have their records made public. Lewis and Clark, for example, kept their diaries as records of official actions. Others, like Samuel Cole Davis, wrote diaries in the hope that the intimacy and intensity of the form would make their statements more moving and credible. Still others, who were endeavoring to make a career from their writings, chose to make use of the advantages of the diary process to develop works in other genres for public view. Although most of these writers intended to keep their journals private or open to only a select group of friends and relations, they were conscious that their records could become an important source for public productions.

A quantitative division of diaries by percentages of the public and private material they contain is less accurate and, therefore, less useful than one that recognizes the multiple qualitative factors that may define a diarist's expectations about audience and the way such factors affect the nature of personal records. This division is particularly important in the American diary literature of this period, but it does affect other diaries.

After reading thousands of diaries I have reached the conclusion that there is no such thing as a totally private diary. I am inclined to believe that almost all, if not all, diarists envision an audience for their entries. Even those diarists who have claimed to be writing for themselves, even those who would profess horror at the idea that anyone else might see their "private confessions," have been writing to an audience. This audience may be an idealized self, a future self, a partial self, but it is not the diarist. A careful reader may find that even in the most "private" diaries the writer has been reluctant or unable to admit thoughts and beliefs to the superconscious "audience" envisioned for the work. Lord Byron wrote in his own diary, "I fear one lies more to one's self than to anyone else," and the discovery and analysis of such self-deceptions are important to the criticism of diary literature.

In talking about the public versus the private diary, the best we can do is to talk about the degree to which the diarist envisions encountering others who have read his/her diary. Not only is the possibility of a future audience just one of the many factors that influence the nature of a diary, but it is not really a single factor. The notion of a continuum of expectation from totally private to totally public is an oversimplification compressing a series of factors into a single one. Even those diarists who expressed their intentions to share their records with others, had varied reasons for and attitudes toward that sharing and, consequently, its influence toward the work. Moreover, even within a diary the attitude of author to audience is rarely constant. The audience that a diarist envisions changes with time, and even where the audience remains constant, a diarist may exhibit a change in attitude toward that audience, so that the material being recorded and the process of diary keeping itself often change radically. It is useful to recognize that factors related to audience do influence diary production; but, as a result of these complex components of the nature and degree of privacy, it is impossible to propose more than very general principles that have any wide application.

The diaries of Ralph Waldo Emerson and A. Bronson Alcott show how difficult it is to evaluate the degree to which a diary is public. Each diary was both public and private. Emerson used his personal record as a place to collect ideas and to work on drafts for publication; and, as his public reception increased, so did the likelihood that the thoughts and language he developed on the pages of the diary would find their way into print. However, his control over audience access to the original did not change; and, therefore, many of his frankest expressions, those most clearly private, were written after the diary's public use had become apparent. Had his diary become more or less public? Alcott did not write his regular diary with the intention of publication, but he repeatedly encouraged his friends and family to read it. Which diary was more "private," Emerson's or Alcott's?

The answers to such questions must begin with the recognition that as a diary habit becomes established, the diary takes on a life of its own. A comparison between original diary material and those sections revised for publication offers useful data to show how a work changed as the conception of audience changed, but such comparisons suggest that it is not the actual exposure to an audience or the size of that audience that is most important. There comes a point at which a diarist can no longer make the diary more private or more public. The personality of the diary has become its own audience. That personality may be affected by the expectation of an outside audience, but it is this perceived entity of the diary that determines the nature of the work.

The Problems of Classification

The difficulty of determining the public/private dimension of diaries is just one of the problems in classifying the diaries that were written in nineteenth-century America. Another is the multiplicity and complexity of motives for diary production that resulted in the multiplicity and complexity of diary forms. As life-styles become more diverse and complex the identification and labeling of the controlling motive often become less clear. With new activities come new types of situation diaries that are similar to or overlap other categories.

One example of the difficulty in distinguishing diary forms is the fine line between the categories of political diary and diplomatic diary. The diaries of diplomats are often a response to the diplomat's assignment to a foreign post and in such cases are more appropriately considered as a form of travel diary than as a political diary, which is determined by its author's response to his/her occupation. Among the distinctions that will be discussed in subsequent chapters are those between the diary of travel and the diary of exploration, the traditional spiritual journal and the journals of the Transcendentalists, and diaries of situation and life diaries. Most of these problems are present in the analysis of colonial American diaries, but making appropriate distinctions is much more difficult in dealing with the diaries written during the nineteenth century.

Chapter Two
Spiritual Journals

Spiritual journals continued to be an important part of American diary literature in the nineteenth century, as Americans continued to recognize the diary as a means to externalize their religious concerns without prematurely exposing those concerns to public scrutiny. Writers still used spiritual journals both to meditate on spiritual concerns and to examine their actions in the light of their religious faiths. However, the spiritual journals of this period are not as important a part of the genre as they are in that of the colonial period.

Part of this change is attributable to the greater diversity of nineteenth-century society. As the society's interests and activities became more numerous and varied, the proportion of diaries devoted to spiritual concerns declined. Another factor was a decline in the importance of religion in American life and in the religious enthusiasm of Americans. Puritan spiritual journals had been one of the most important types of colonial diary. However, the descendants of the Puritans lacked the religious commitment of their ancestors, whose faith had prompted their migration to the New World and continued to influence all of their actions. Many of them had changed or abandoned the religion of their ancestors. One sign of this development was the rise of Unitarianism and the subsequent development of American Transcendentalism. Just as many of the American Transcendentalists of this period could trace their ancestry to the Puritans, so their journals, discussed later in this work, are related to Puritan spiritual journals.

A significant exception to the decline of the religious spiritual journal in this period is the Quaker spiritual diary. While none of the early nineteenth-century Quaker spiritual journals can challenge John Woolman's eighteenth-century journal, Woolman's was only partially a diary; a large part of its material was revised into autobiography proper. However, among the early nineteenth-century Quaker diaries are a number of excellent works that are all or primarily true diaries.

One of the reasons the Quakers of the early nineteenth century continued to create these spiritual diaries may be the central role of divine inspiration in their religion. Certainly Quaker spiritual journals seem to have retained a great deal of the religious enthusiasm evident in earlier spiritual journals. Another reason may be the Quaker tradition of using journals as a means of publicly expressing their faith. Among the best of these Quaker spiritual journals are those of Samuel Cole Davis and Charles Osborn.

The Diary of Samuel Cole Davis (1764–1809)

With the exception of a brief prefatory entry, the diary of Samuel Cole Davis covers a period of less than eighteen months. But the regularity and length of those entries make the volume substantial. The reason for this extraordinary period of diary production was that, during the time of its composition, Davis was dying of cancer. This disease provided the motivation for his attempt to resolve a number of long-standing personal problems as well as the more immediate ones that resulted from the cancer itself. As a Quaker, his problems involved not merely the ordering of his earthly affairs at the end of his physical life, but also the ordering of his spiritual state in preparation for eternity. The prospect of facing death would by itself go far in making a diary interesting; but when, as is the case with the Davis diary, this content is matched by a controlling form, the result is a work of special value.

It is rare for a diarist to have so clear a sense of audience. Davis's diary was intended to help its author to solve certain specific problems; however, Davis was writing not only for himself, some imaginary confidant, or a specific friend or relation. Instead, with an awareness of the Quaker spiritual journal as a special form, he directed his words to a wider audience. He even went so far as to address the reader directly, offering his life and insights as spiritual guides. But, significantly, Davis as a diarist rather than an autobiographer had no assurance as to where his narrative would lead. His journal is not like that of a returned explorer telling of his successfully completed adventure, but rather like that of the protagonist of Poe's "Manuscript Found in a Bottle," the account of a shipwrecked wanderer who has almost abandoned hope of his own physical survival but who still keeps an account of his last voyage into the unknown for the benefit of an audience he does not expect ever to meet.

This concern for audience is a very special characteristic of Quaker spiritual diaries. Most American spiritual diaries, in the tradition of the Puritan spiritual diary, are very private documents. For the Puri-

tans and their descendants the spiritual diary and the spiritual autobiography had several similar features but distinctly different roots.
The Puritan spiritual journal is most closely related to the Puritan's
arduous search for grace. Indeed, it was often relied on as the sole
companion in that effort. In seeking salvation the Puritan was alone.
The autobiographical confession, like the public declaration of sin that
was part of the Puritan's petition for church membership, also included
the petitioner's belief in his or her election to a state of grace. Rejecting
as "popish" heresy the use of any earthly mediator in attaining salvation, the Puritan eschewed public involvement in the process. A diary
like Michael Wigglesworth's with its frequent declarations of sin and
rare announcements of success was not written with any expectation
that it would become public. Autobiographies such as Jonathan Edwards's may speak of sin, but they carry the assurance of salvation.
Doubt was not often made public; David Brainerd had removed and
destroyed a section of his journal treating his early years of spiritual
uncertainty before he allowed it to be edited for publication. The public confession of sin of which Dimmesdale's fictional example in *The
Scarlet Letter* is the most widely known took place in a moment not of
despair but of achievement, and is therefore more closely related to
autobiography proper.

Early Quakers such as Davis had both the Quaker meeting with its
open participation by the assembled Friends and the model of their
founder George Fox as guides, suggesting the parallel public natures
of both the religious process and the diary. For Quakers the line between diary and autobiography proper, if acknowledged, was relatively
unimportant. For example, a large part of *The Journal of John Woolman,*
the most famous of all the American Quaker autobiographies, is diary
material. Theology as well as practice further contributed to this situation. Instead of feeling helpless in dealing with sin, the Quaker had
a conviction that a direct and personal relationship to God was possible
if he followed the divine Light within him. Davis's attempt to follow
these divine promptings not only provided material for the diary, but
shaped its presentation.

Like his religion, Davis's illness influenced both the form and the
content of his diary. As time passed, the increasing severity of Davis's
symptoms made death, the necessary limit on the work, seem that
much closer. At first, Davis hoped for a recovery, praying for God's
mercy and declaring with every sign of remission that he would seize
on this return to health as an opportunity to lead a life in accordance
with divine principles:

I think the Lord had a regard to any petition in regard to a desire that I had
concerning how I would wish to spend my days daily if ever I should ever be
recovered of this disease, or if I never do experience a recovery.

. . . I have been favored to spend my time in a good degree profitably.
This I think I certainly know, for when ever I lay down to take a night's rest
by taking a strict examination of all my conduct of the preceding or past day
and finding all to speak peace, then all things feel agreeable to the mind.[1]

While such hopes existed, Davis might view his work like his life as
essentially open-ended. Therefore, the development of the diary's
equivalent of "plot" and the various "themes" it advanced would move
forward slowly. Yet, from the first, Davis had a presentiment that the
disease would be fatal and that the time allotted to him should be spent
in remedying old failings rather than in pleading for new opportunities. In the Quaker tradition of personal revelation, this presentiment
came in the form of a spiritual visitation:

Laying down on my bed I thought I perceived an audible or belief voice[2] which
seemed plain to my ears saying, "Oh Samuel, consider the duration of Eternity. Why should thee fret and get into passions and use bad language when
dressing thy sore? Remember it was the Lord that sent this affliction on thee?
I then thought I would take up a resolution, let what should be the event to
submit to my fate with as much patience and as strong a resolution to do
better.[3]

Six months later Davis had a similar experience. First sensing his
own sinfulness and recognizing that he might be "cut off in the middle
or midst of . . . [his] days as an unprofitable servant" (11/17/08), he
made the first of several declarations that his disease was a blessing in
that it worked for his soul's benefit: "I seriously thinking that it is my
greatest good, and that he is willing to give me an opportunity to make
a lasting peace with him, and O may this affliction prove to be the
greatest blessing I ever received, and it should be the will of my Heavenly Father to heal this disease and spare me yet a little longer" (11/
17/08). But here, as in other early entries, "progress" toward the acceptance of God and the rejection of earthly goals became twisted into
a renewed hope for physical life, an attitude that shows that his concern
was still for the flesh and not for the spirit. As the entry continues,
Davis tells of another vision that came to correct his error:

I was going to say a few years longer, and I at this time did desire to be spared
a few years longer . . . to have made amendment of life in future visibly to

be known of all my acquaintance. But in the visions of the night of the 18th
. . . I saw with my spiritual eyes, a hand who plainly pointed out to me and
said, "Desire not to live a few years; for it won't be granted to thee; but thee
may be spared a little time longer; so thee may try to be in readiness against
. . . thy appointed time to die. Ever since the above night, I have set my
whole heart to study how to get in readiness and to strive to have my past
sinful life pardoned so I may be at peace with my maker before I die and go
hence and am seen of man no more in this world of trouble. (11/17/08)

As the diary developed, Davis moved further and further from a
concern for continued life and the world of matter and closer to the
acceptance of death and a concern for the things of the spirit. While
this movement is evident, it is not consistent either in speed or in
direction; as a ball that has rolled off a table bounces lower and lower
before coming to rest, so Davis occasionally reached for life even as he
moved steadily toward death and a "willingness" to die (12/4/08). This
pattern is one of several elements that give the diary its form.

This movement can be studied by examining Davis's concern for his
sins. At first he was concerned with sin as an active present option,
writing in the diary his belief that the disease was providential in that,
by making him aware of death, it prompted him to strive to live properly and that by incapacitating him it kept him from committing "such
horrible sins" and stopped his "sad career in sin" (10/8/08). Even when
he would lie to a neighbor, his fear of dying "with a new fault" (12/
23/08) soon induced him to seek God's forgiveness and to promise
never knowingly to sin. By such means he was led to conclude, "this
affliction may prove to be a blessing and that it may be profitable to
my soul" (10/2/08). Thus the illness became converted from the cause
of misery to the alleviation of it:

Oh that I could set forth to the world the goodness of the Lord and the tender
mercies that he hath bestowed to me a vile and unworthy sinner; for he is
daily affording to me every day, yea methinks more evident favors than some
thousands do enjoy in that he hath not cut my life off in the midst of my sins
and grievous provocations against him, my now only comforter under this
heavy affliction that he hath suffered to come on me, but we all must die and
we know not when or how or what may hasten it. . . . Except he had thus
warned me to repent I would have been most miserable. (5/4/09)

Recognizing that the awareness of pain and sin could be the means to
their extinction, Davis came to view that awareness as opportunity. In

this way he eagerly sought occasions to pay attention to his past flaws and present suffering.

Davis's present avoidance of sin was not sufficient to convince him that he had attained grace because the awareness of death also made him sensitive to the fact that he needed to redeem those sins already committed. His newfound ability to confront his past aided him in this task: "This day I felt uneasy in my mind, with hearty desires to know while here if the Lord will be pleased to guide me aright and enable me to give my whole heart up unto him; I abhor all my past life of sin at this time as much as ever I loved to live in sin—pardon me O Lord for my past offenses, for I feel sick of the thoughts of how I used to lead my life in sin" (11/27/08). As the thoughts of his misdeeds would "pain" and "pester," Davis searched his life to come to grips with them. "Conversing" with his heart, he began to find those threads that led from his past sins to his future redemption (12/4/08).

Davis even prepared a long autobiographical passage, beginning with details of his birth and pious upbringing but moving soon to an examination of his departure from the devout Quaker standards of his parents and to his recent sinful life. Tracing his sin to the period following his marriage, Davis concluded that it was then that through association with "unprofitable company" he began to drink excessively and indulge his taste for fashionable clothes and expensive possessions. However, even earlier he had been allowed and even aided in his movement away from God and toward a dissolute life by the leniency of an overindulgent father. One specific instance that Davis cited in support of such a conclusion was the time when he persuaded his father to buy him "a fine riding horse . . . which proved to be a smart race horse."[4] Recollection of this indulgent act prompted Davis to make one of several attempts in the diary to warn parents against such leniency.

Davis's tendency to blame others for his sins was an important facet of his personality, and one sign of his development during the composition of the diary is his growing ability to accept blame. One step toward such an acceptance of blame was his acknowledgment that he was more aware of his actions than he had previously admitted. He acknowledged that, prior to his illness, awareness that his actions were causing mental distress for his friends and family never caused him sufficient anguish to make him turn aside from his course of behavior.

In the diary Davis revealed a tendency for contentiousness which affected his relationships with neighbors and relatives. Most of the disputes that Davis mentioned in the diary were tempered by his attempts to correct this character flaw, but the tone of the halfhearted forgiveness that he offered in many of these accounts shows Davis's difficulty in achieving self-reform. For example, in a single passage he condemned his stepbrother as a "deceiver" before offering pardon (5/6/ 09). Of a dispute with one Joseph Boroughs, Davis wrote that he freely forgave him, although such forgiveness seemed "hard and unnatural" (6/8/09). In another entry he revealed the conflicting impulses in his character:

My pretended friends would carry a deaf ear to all my complaints so that by this usage I seemed to be almost beside reason, and I became uneasy and fretful, so that unguardedly I began to get outrageous and to my great sorrow of heart did use such hard and wicked speeches and threats to my own brother as is not fit for mortal man to use or utter out of any one's mouth. Besides, I said I were in a good mind or I would make way with my life, but I did not intend to do it as I fear the judgments of the Lord would be hard on me if I did—my friends as I thought then seemed all to join against my proceedings, and refused me even money enough for the ease of the sore, but I do seriously forgive them all their hardness to me, and do earnestly desire and pray to the Lord my comforter to forgive me of this my great sin and wickedness, for it is and hath been a great trouble on my mind for so doing this day the sore was very easy as to hard pains. (5/6/09)

This passsage suggests that while Davis may not always have been fully aware of the implications of his words and deeds, he was at least partially conscious of them. His own words suggest that he realized that his behavior might have given his friends cause to doubt his sanity and so may have made their harsh treatment of him excusable, but Davis still persisted in calling them "pretended friends" who stood in need of his pardon. This passage also reveals the complex relationship between Davis's physical state, or at least the suffering he felt from his disease, and his efforts at improving his spiritual state. When Davis was able to make even a partial admission of his misbehavior, his eased conscience was matched by an eased pain.

    This complex process by which Davis's personal relationships, self-awareness, spiritual state, and disease interacted is especially noticeable in those entries in which he wrote about his relationship with his wife. His disease and the resulting spiritual awakening which the diary chronicles caused major changes in his approach to that relationship. In an early entry Davis confessed his sinful nature, admitting that he had been "very cruel and crossly inclined" to his wife "often times for no real cause only for provocation and strife" and begged forgiveness (11/2/08). Even when he wrote that she has been "overtaken with that evil practice of taking too much strong drink," he tried to avoid recriminations and instead to express concern for her salvation. Such an attitude was a significant improvement from his earlier behavior; however, the reader of the diary is likely to suspect that such pardon as Davis offered in these entries may have been tainted by pride in some new sense of holiness. It was not until the closing section of the diary period, as death came close, that Davis was able to move from this limited forgiveness of others to the acceptance of his own culpability in these personal relationships.

In one of these later entries Davis expressed his realization that the origin of sin was internal and that it ran counter to, rather than resulted from, the actions of others. Moving from an admission of his youthful indiscretions of lying, disobedience, and general mischief, Davis acknowledged that this early pattern continued in his adult life. He admitted "swearing and drinking to excess and quarrelsome jealousy between my wife and others for no grounds except listening to what people said of her concerning he who also had no better credit." Accepting his own guilt, Davis could finally see the hypocrisy and ultimate futility of his previous attempts to deal with his sin. He would, he admitted, "stifle" guilt with drink, and even when he felt "heavy convictions for sin," these would not lead to spiritual purification or even improved behavior, but rather to promises to God as false as those he had made to his wife (7/8/09).

These admissions of hypocrisy led to Davis's ultimate realization about his sinful life. In a climactic entry or rather a series of entries— for in this section the entries give only the month and not the individual day—Davis was finally able to name his greatest sin. Even here he could only work up to his confession by stages. He began the entry with an address to the reader that announced his good intentions:

Dearly beloved young people, I who am a person who always loved good will and harmony to dwell between a man and his wife or any others in regard of having of any thoughts of jealousy to appear as it is a ruinous thing in the world to be jealous in any thing, therefore, I do wish to set forth openly to the world and before all the neighborhood of my acquaintance that, as I have a sincere desire to repent of all the sins I have committed in my knowledge, one important thing that has been clearly shown to me this night is that as I had I thought real cause to be jealous of my dear wife whom I seriously loved, and I really thought her to have been guilty of cohabitting with many other men, but with the sorrow of heavens I do confess not to have been guilty of the charge laid against her, and I had no real foundation to think any such thing of her, but it hath been nothing short of as I had a mind to have lived a chaste and upright life with her to the end; but I think it was a suggestion of Satan who hath led me to believe it to be the truth and harkening too much to loose idle tales which were told me in order to see what I would say. (7/12/09)

Here Davis directed his attention to depersonalized jealousy. Associating it with Adam's fall, "The first and great grand cause of disobedience and beginning of desolation in the world with all the race of mankind," Davis was able to place the blame for his sin on Satan, the "grand enemy of our souls" (7/12/09). However, as the entry was continued, its author shifted the blame away from the Devil and toward his own willingness to believe in those false accusations. Although, at this point, Davis was still portraying himself as a passive sinner "forced . . . with the help of drinking to excess," through the admission of these sins, he finally came to make a crucial admission: "These above lines I have written in order to show you what I now confess to believe, and also to show you that I myself have been guilty of that horrid sin of committing adultery. So I have been the worst of us both as far as I know" (7/12/09).

Recognizing this mechanism of projecting his own sins upon others, Davis was able to find his illness both a deserved and apt punishment and his life an important example to others. As he had never been thankful to God for his many blessings or restrained his "appetite from any good thing which I could procure to myself be it ever so costly and rare," so he would now accept God's visitation of a disease that made all tastes repugnant and all living painful (7/12/09). God, he concluded, had been merciful because the suffering that He visited upon Davis had brought a late but timely repentance and consequently a hope for salvation. Davis could then declare his situation to be preferable to those of his anticipated readers if they failed to heed his example.

In describing his disease, Davis offered nauseatingly repugnant images: The nose "wasting away," the teeth and gums "eaten out and going to leave the bones bare" (7/12/09); but like the burning spider's death that Jonathan Edwards described in his famous sermon "Sinners in the Hands of An Angry God," the fearful image was transformed into something promising. As Edwards argued that God did not cast men into hell, but rather for a time kept them up from a fate that their own sin was earning them, so Davis found his suffering was not God's punishment, but the outward manifestation of his own iniquity. The fact that he had been kept from death during his lingering illness showed Davis "the necessity of having all my support and desires unto the almighty providence of God to support and keep me at all times" (7/12/09).

With this conviction he could now warn his readers not to do as he had done in delaying his search for divine pardon. In giving this advice, Davis was not the saved man sure that in the face of death he sees truth, but the suffering sinner who would spare others from the harshness of his fate. Indeed, in noting that he wished his diary or some portion of it published so that it might have some good effect, he felt it necessary to warn:

Don't let any one part of what you see written in this book tend to deceive or mislead your minds to think I am what I am not; neither wholly put a firm dependence on what is written in some parts of this book, as I confess I had not a real sense and fielding [*sic*] of what I wrote but it sprang from the willingness of discouraging of others from doing as I did and from desires to discouraging vice and immorality from getting the sway of anyone's affections. I believe if this book is kept in remembrance it may if rightly understood for what end it was written that it may be of some use to discourage others from pursuing such dreadful wicked practices; O the great need and necessity there is in leading a serious and godly life. . . . I have in some parts of this book wrote of some things and not been attended to in the right spirit; but I was in a degree easy on the mind and of a hidden spirit in me of lukewarmness and was too self-righteous and sure of redemption and pardon, and now at times see it to have been the case with myself but now I can't say any good of myself but feel all poor and incapable of doing or saying of any good thing. I am nothing, nothing of myself, but want everyone to lay it to heart for themselves and take warning by any wretchedness, nothing in me to be good but the spirit of grace. (7/14/09)

By offering such a warning Davis was consciously choosing between the diary form and that of autobiography proper. The retention of his early entries intact, despite the fact that they expressed views that he had come to feel he had outgrown, was an act of faith. This faith was multiple. Of course, it included a total faith in God to replace his lost faith in his own capacity, but it also represented faith in the diary form itself. The elements of this faith were a trust in the reader to distinguish between what Davis believed was his early egotism and what he came to feel was his new submission of self and a trust in the diary form to reveal truth through partial truth or even complete falsehood, especially through the falsehood of premature security, which mistakes the first hope for divine mercy as accomplished repentance. These faiths were linked because to trust in the changing reality of the daily record was to trust in life itself as a process. Faith in the diary form denies both an existential insistance on the individual moment and the simple balancing of all good and evil acts. Instead, it suggests that life is a process that, though best done well throughout, may be acceptable if it leads to the right end.

Charles Osborn (1775–1850)

Osborn's diary begins on January 12, 1809, shortly after he and a companion had left on a "religious visit" to Friends in North Carolina. The diary may have been prompted by the difficulties he encountered early in that trip not only from "a good many apparent dangers and considerable hardship and fatigue" occasioned by the winter weather, but also by his limited success in his work. Osborn did note that he had been "received kindly" by the Friends of that region, and occasional signs of divine favor through which "Truth reigned over all"; however, he more frequently complained that many a "glorious opportunity" went unrealized. He spoke of "hard labor" and "a distressing time to our minds."[5]

In one entry he wrote of a dark moment that occurred while he was speaking at a meeting: "all at once I was stopped by a cloud of dreadful darkness which came over me. The like I think I had never felt. It seemed the air looked gloomy before me. I sat down under great discouragement"(5). This image of a "cloud of darkness" was just the first of a number of similar experiences recorded in the journal. On one level they serve to show Osborn's tendency to periods of severe depression; on another they symbolize a special form of religious experience. Osborn came to find that God would as often direct him through the impeding force of these depressions and the relief of their removal than by religious experiences that would exalt him above the ordinary.[6]

Finally Osborn began to have some successes. In calling one such "victory, contrary to the expectations of some present, who were not willing to believe that 'Charles Osborn' had any mission to preach," he seems to have been addressing his own misgivings as well as those of these doubters (7). He did not take credit for these successes but repeatedly emphasized in his journal that all of his achievements were the work of God: "Lord! all is from thee. I am a poor worm" (49). Osborn was increasingly able to note occasions when he was able to surprise those "who, looking upon me as man looketh, were ready to conclude that it was impossible for such a man as Charles Osborn to preach" so that they were amazed and struck with wonder as he "livingly declared the truths of the gospel" (12). By 1810 he was convinced of his calling and realized that he would have to leave his family to "travel in the service of the Lord" (13). He continued to have occasional moments of doubt during which he would "feel altogether unable to speak in the name of the Lord, as I did when I first began," but more usually he felt satisfied of his success (40).

Osborn frequently felt torn between what he felt was a divinely or-dained command to travel in God's service and his personal desire to stay with his family, a dilemma that was particularly acute after the death of his first wife and his remarriage. However, in January 1814 Osborn felt another command to make a visit to North Carolina, South Carolina, and Georgia. On February 20, after his own meeting had declined to give advice that would free him from the obligation he felt, Osborn left.

On that trip Osborn had a particularly distressing experience, an early indication of what would later have an important effect on his life:

—traveled six miles and put up at the house of a slaveholder—a rich planter. He received us kindly and treated us well, not charging us anything. I conceived that this man would well bear the appellation of "merciful tyrant." His slaves appeared in good clothing, and something like folks in their manners, yet they are deprived of the most precious of all jewels, liberty. This must be tyranny if there is anything under the whole heavens which will bear that appellation. When will the time come when Christians will be Christians, and treat their fellow men, for which Christ died, as brethren? (91)

In his record of this trip Osborn noted his meetings with individuals from many different groups. Some were sympathetic, offering hospitality and attention to his view, others less obliging or congenial. One of the more interesting of these encounters was that with a group of Shakers. He found them friendly, inviting him and his companion to dinner and caring for their horses; however, he explained that despite their "show of kindness," he "felt something dark and disagreeable to oppose . . . [his] mind." Osborn became particularly distressed when, upon talking with the Shaker elders, he learned of their doctrines of sanctification and celibacy and their refusal to let him conduct a meeting among them (99-100).

One of Osborn's periods of depression came during a visit to Philadelphia:[7]

I was prevented from making any effort to leave the city, by a cloud of darkness which came upon me, not to be described, at least not to the full. My judgment was so taken away, that I found myself on the brink of the awful gulf of dispair. I saw I could not move. In vain did my friends attempt to add to my comfort. I retired, laid down, turned my face to the wall, and remembered king Hezekiah, who in like position wept sore. (147)

Osborn's depression finally lifted when a member of the ministry of a nearby town invited him to come there and helped him to see that his mission would not be complete until he had held meetings at the State Prison and the Poor House. As a result of his experience Osborn concluded that the "dark cloud" was an act of the Lord who "even in judgment . . . exercisest mercy" (148)

On several occasions Osborn wrote of being "so exceedingly loaded with exercises and sorrow" that he feared that his "mental faculties are somewhat impaired." These depressions would occur even when he could claim that "I am not sensible that I have done anything to wound my own conscience" (161). Declaring himself "a poor creature" in need of "grace, daily to direct my steps," Osborn found it extremely "sweet" and "pleasant" to examine his actions during a day and find none "the remembrance of which produces condemnation" (157–58). This search for transgressions or exemption from blame may have been one of the motives for his journalizing.

Most of Osborn's journal is written during periods in which he traveled for his faith. Over one third of the extant record covers his religious visit to Great Britain, Ireland, France, Germany, Switzerland, and the Netherlands in 1832 and 1833. On March 13, 1832 Osborn left his home,[8] wife, and children for what he called his "apprehended duty" to serve God (233, 253). On April 8 he sailed from New York on the *Silas Richards* bound for Liverpool.

Though he could praise the almost excessive kindness of the English Friends, Osborn was disappointed that their lives failed to follow the example set by those English Friends of an earlier period whose writings had inspired him (228–29). He came to conclude that while many

American Friends had drifted away from what he considered the true principles of his faith by denying matters of doctrine such as "the divinity of Jesus Christ" and by placing too much stress on "the light and spirit within," the English Friends had "gone off on the other side, placing too much on the atonement, and exalting the scripture as the primary rule of faith and practice" (292). One special disappointment occurred when Osborn went to the former residence of George Fox, founder of the Society of Friends, at Swarthmore and found that there were "few Friends to meet there now" (271).

However, a greater disappointment for Osborn was his own initial inability to fulfill his expectations for himself. At first humbled at being unable to do the work he desired, Osborn at last found his voice. While attending a meeting, he felt the Lord suddenly make him stand to expound on a passage of scripture and then lead him on "clothed . . . with gospel power which reached the hearts of most, if not all present" (230–31). Osborn continued to have occasional successes of this sort, but at least as often he talked of weeping in secret over his spiritual state or his own inability to do God's work. He felt particularly hampered on the continent of Europe, where despite the advantage of an interpreter he felt constrained by his own inability to speak the language of those he sought to influence.

Finally Osborn set off for America, landing in New York on July 31, 1833, and arriving home on September 3. Osborn continued to keep journals after his return but the surviving volumes suggest that he no longer kept up the practice to the extent that he had earlier.

A number of his last entries, part of a short volume he kept in the final year of his life, are concerned with the issue of slavery. The entry about the slaveholding Quaker cited above is only one of a number of earlier entries that show his concern about this issue was a long-standing one. Nevertheless, his concern appears to have grown much stronger over time.[9] He seems to have been motivated by congressional actions that, he declared, "cannot fail to bring additional infamy and reproach upon the people of our whole nation." Seeing the "high standard of American liberty . . . fallen prostrate before the demon of slavery . . . the rights of heaven invaded, and important Christian duties made crimes," he suggested that Washington had become "Satan's seat" (469) and that the supporters of slavery could not be true Friends. He certainly accepted Woolman's practice of refusing to support slaveholders or to use items created by slave labor, going so far as to claim that those who were "in the practice of voting for military chieftains, slaveholders and Pro-Slavery men" or who "used the products of the poor degraded, down-trodden, lash driven slaves," could not "expect to have favored meetings" (471).

Osborn's final entry was written on November 24, 1850, only a little over a month before his death. Although unwell, he wrote that "being favored to have my mind staid upon God, I have peace." Perhaps before he died he experienced periods of depression, and even when writing this final entry he may not have achieved "perfect peace" any more than he had earlier in his life; but, as he explained in the entry he wrote the day before, "Though I am not without trials and poverty of spirit, yet . . . I have cause for rejoicing: for the cup of unmixed felicity is not a draught for mortals, if it were, where would be the reserve for futurity?" (471–72).

Other Spiritual Journals

There are many other early nineteenth-century American spiritual journals worthy of attention. Included in these are some that help to put Davis's and Osborn's in perspective. Those who wish to read more of these works would be well advised to consider the journals of Catherine Seely and Mildred Ratcliff.

Seely's journal can be compared to Davis's; both diarists were motivated to seek religious fulfillment because of their experiences with illness. In one entry Seely described a dream that, she concluded, presented "a true picture of my recent sickness." In the dream she "stood on a high precipice, beneath which was eternity," while a net pulled her "with an irresistible impulse toward the brink." Before she could be cast down she perceived herself "rescued through the unmeritted mercy of Jehovah, and permitted to go free for a while to finish . . . [her] preparation for that great change."[10] In a later entry she compared a period of sickness to "a small boat on the boisterous ocean, subject to constant changes," her "slender bark . . . often . . . sunk beneath the foaming waves of disease and pain" (47).

Mildred Ratcliff's journal is more like that of Osborn though less unified and more repetitive. Born a Baptist, Ratcliff not only accepted her husband's Quaker faith, but became a "public advocate" of that religion, traveling and speaking as Osborn did. Ratcliff's public support for her faith and her reputation as a "prophetess and discerner of spirits" brought her widespread regard. Osborn not only knew of her and her work but, in his journal for April 12, 1820, mentioned meeting her (she does not mention him in her entry).

Her journal includes a large number of entries describing her travels in the service of her religion; in these entries she talks of God in the third person. For example, she wrote about how her confidence in God overcame her fear about crossing a "rapid stream": "While we waited on the shore, my mind turned inward, I felt renewed evidence of his care, and that I need not be dismayed at the foaming deep; for that we in safety should pass over it."[11] In other entries she addressed God in the first person, and her entry became a prayer:

I take my pen in hand whilst the rest are in bed. It seems to be the only quiet time I can get of late to do this part of my day's work; which, O my father, I am almost out of heart of ever accomplishing. . . . O Lord my God! Thou knowest I am weak, and my enemies are strong. . . . If Thou my Father withdraw thyself from me, I shall fall by the hand of my enemy. (76)

As the entry suggests, Ratcliff considered diary keeping to be an important part of her religious duties.

Chapter Three
Diaries of Travel and Exploration

Many diaries have their origins in simpler, less personal forms such as weather records, business accounts, and the like. However, there are some basic diary types that tend to lead a writer directly into the processes necessary for a true diary. The spiritual journal is one such type. But the most common is the diary of travel or exploration. The primary impulse for most diary production is an imbalance, disorder, or dislocating change in the world of its author, and diaries are perceived as creative and positive attempts to resolve the tension between the current or anticipated state and a more familiar or desirable one. As the "surface" dislocations of travel and exploration are so obvious and so open to anticipation, it should not be particularly surprising that the works that they inspire constitute one of the most common forms of diary. So compelling is the dislocation of travel that the concerns and experiences it prompts may take over and redirect an already established diary-keeping pattern.

The extent of this dislocation has changed with time. With the exception of such periods as the "Dark Ages," there has been a steady increase in the speed of travel, the effectiveness of communication, and the homogeneity of culture. The unfamiliar and the unknown were closer in the past than they are today. Consequently, in the past travelers were more likely to be affected by new experiences than are modern travelers. Even those early nineteenth-century American diarists who traveled in the sections of the world that had long since been explored and settled were likely to bring home accounts that would seem novel. This fact may help to explain the enormous popularity of travel literature in the period.

Diaries of the Frontier

Contrary to commonsense expectation, Americans "were travelers before they were explorers."[1] In the colonial period Americans thinking of the future looked east toward Europe. Eastward lay the positive values: civilization, culture, and reason; westward lay the negatives: savagery, ignorance, and bestiality. However, in the beginning of the nineteenth century the compass of American attitudes underwent a shift in polarity. East became the direction of the old, the stale, the antiquated; while West became the new, the vital, and the original.

There was a corresponding shift in diary literature. American colonists wrote many more good diaries of travel than diaries of exploration; however, in the first half of the nineteenth century the citizens of the new American nation produced a large number of excellent exploration diaries. In part this shift was the result of the new sense of national identity that resulted from the Revolution; in part it was the influence of Romanticism, which exalted the wild, the natural, and the primitive.

These diaries of the frontier were not only the product of a change in attitude, they were also a factor in the spread of that change. Many were widely read, and inspired others to explore and to admire the spirit of exploration.

The Lewis and Clark Expedition (1804–1806) Meriwether Lewis (1774–1809) & William Clark (1770–1838)

The Lewis and Clark expedition was an achievement of monumental proportions, for it involved not only the heroic effort of the men in the expedition, but also the faith of the American people in their future. The achievement supported the American claim to expansion to the Pacific and served as a prophecy of the thousands of journeys west that would follow. The diaries of this expedition were read by Americans not only as an indication of what had been done, but also of what would be done. They form a vital part of the diary literature of America.

The number and length of the diary record of the expedition are proportionate to its achievement. It is possible that as many as nine members of the official party kept diaries, six of which—those of Captains Meriwether Lewis and William Clark; Sergeants Charles Floyd, Patrick Gass, and John Ordway; and Private John Whitehouse—have been published.[2] In addition there is a version of the work authorized by Clark and written by Nicholas Biddle from the original materials made available to him; it is this version that has been most widely published and read. Biddle's abbreviated composite is, of course, not a "pure" diary, but it is more a diary than anything else, preserving the form, perspective, and much of the language of the original.

Even the original diaries were not totally "pure." The diarist-explorers wrote most of their accounts in moments of leisure at camp from notes made while traveling; and, at these times, some of them copied material written by others into their own records. To complicate this situation further, these "field books" were, in turn, rewritten after the explorers returned (1:xxxiv–xxxv). In attempting to deal with such a large and complex set of materials, it is not easy to make critical judgments; and it is always necessary to make a careful determination of which materials are being considered before making any evaluation. A number of editions are available, and the reader's choice will depend on the intended use of the diary.[3]

The size and complexity of these diaries makes it impractical, if not impossible, to attempt in this book the same type of analysis applied to most of the other journals; moreover, the nature of this body of materials makes it less likely that such an effort would be productive. Jefferson, the president who conceived and ordered the expedition, instructed the explorers to keep a record so that they might preserve notes on points of navigation, the identity and characteristics of the Indian nations, matters of zoological, botanical, and meteorological interest, and several other subjects. The attempt to carry out these instructions faithfully, combined with the pressures from time and situation, could only have helped to shape the works in ways antithetical to the expectations of literary art. The concerns and achievements of art are not altogether absent, but they appear in larger and less focused patterns than those that can be seen in most diaries.

We can simplify our work by concentrating our attention on the two longest and most significant journals, those of Captains Lewis and Clark. These two documents are linked by common objectives and an interchange of materials during the process of composition. It is desirable to read both because the differences in their authors' experiences and perspectives complement one another and make for a more complete record; however, it is impossible to overlook the fact that Lewis's education and training had equipped him better for writing than had Clark's. Lewis's entries are more fluent and more grammatical, and their superior vocabulary, style, and grammar suggest the utility of his greater reading background. For this reason most of the citations here are from Lewis's contributions.

Much of the record of the expedition was devoted to the fulfillment of its assigned tasks. There are hundreds of pages of detailed descriptions of every new species of plant or animal and each novel geological feature. Hundreds more contain descriptions of the cultures of the various Indian tribes encountered. Most of the rest is filled with well-written but straightforward accounts of the routine actions of the party. Relatively little space is devoted to personal attitudes or even to an overriding sense of the mission. Such material would seem to preclude the creation of a work worthy of literary consideration; and yet a reader opening a volume of the work at random may, forgetful of time, find himself a hundred or more pages into the book. Surely, something is there to captivate the reader's attention and to hold that attention as the work shifts from one topic to another and from one author to another.

What is the force that unifies the work through these shifts? It is, I would suggest, a sense of implicit conflict between these explorers and the wilderness through which they traveled. Lewis and Clark seem never to have been completely comfortable with the primitive world. Even though to accomplish their task they, like the Indians they met, had to assume roles in harmony with the wilderness, these explorers constantly reminded their readers that those roles were only temporary.

Through their journals Lewis and Clark tried to resolve the tension produced by the "novelty" of the wilderness by assuming a scientific pose. Although their expedition ran from 1804 to 1806, Lewis and Clark were creatures of the Enlightenment. There seems to have been no question in their minds that reason and civilization were superior to intuition and nature. Many frontier explorers adapted to the wilderness by accepting primitive attitudes to suit primitive actions, but Lewis and Clark rejected such a shift and imposed their own concept of order on the wilderness.

Totaling in neat columns the hours, minutes, and seconds of a lunar eclipse (1:248), including in a description of a new plant an observation that "the radicles [were] larger than in most fusiform roots"(3:12), or recording their positions as "At our encampment of this evening observed time and distance of $\mathbb{D}^s$ western limb from spica $\eta\chi$ with sextant" (2:8), Lewis and Clark used their knowledge, activity, and vocabulary to show that there was a great gulf between their own world and the one they had entered.

While creating the legends of a new epoch, they were the destroyers of the old. For example, one entry treats the belief of an Indian tribe that a particular conic hill is "the residence of Deavels. . . . in human form with remarkable large heads, and about eighteen inches high, that they are watchful and armed with Sharp arrows with which they Can Kill at a great distance . . . [and who] are Said to kill all persons who are So hardy as to attempt to approach the hill" (1:119). The explorers reported that, having received this warning, they marched to the hill where they exorcised its demons by recording its size, form, and location in their diaries. When they had finished, "the only remarkable Characteristic of this hill" was that it was "insulated or Separated a considerable distance from any other" (1:124).

The power of the wilderness often resisted such conquest. Long before William Faulkner used a bear as a symbol of the untamed wilderness, members of the expedition remarked on the animal's power and ferocity. In the following entry, Lewis wrote of his reaction to an encounter with one:

Bratton had shot him through the center of the lungs, notwithstanding which he had pursued him near half a mile and had returned more than double that distance and with his tallons had prepared himself a bed in the earth of about 2 feet deep and five long and was perfectly alive when we found him which could not have been less than 2 hours after he received the wound; these bear being so hard to die reather intimidated us all; I must confess that I do not like the gentlemen and had reather fight two Indians than one bear. (2:25)

Their dangerous adventures provided exciting episodes such as that in which Clark was nearly swept away by a flash flood "Poreing down the hill in[to] the River with emence force tareing every thing before it takeing with it large rocks & mud" (2:199). In another entry Lewis described a passage across the face of steep bluffs made slippery by recent rains:

In passing along the face of one of these bluffs today I slipped at a narrow pass of about 30 yards in length and but for a quick and fortunate recovery by means of my espontoon I should have been precipitated into the river down a craggy pricipice of about ninety feet. I had scarcely reached a place on which I could stand with tolerable safety even with the assistance of my espontoon before I heard a voice behind me cry out god god Cap! what shall I do on turning about I found it was Windsor who had sliped and fallen ab[o]ut the center of this narrow pass and was lying prostrate on his belley, with his wright hand arm and leg over the precipice while he was holding on with the left arm and foot as well as he could which appeared to be with much difficulty. I discovered his danger and the trepedation which he was in gave me still further concern for I expected every instant to see him loose his strength and slip off; altho' much allarmed at his situation I disguised my feelings and spoke very calmly to him and assured him that he was in no kind of danger, to take the knife out of his belt behind him with his wright hand and dig a hole with it in the face of the bank to receive his wright foot which he did and then raised himself to his knees; I then directed him to take off his mockersons and to come forward on his hands and knees holding the knife in one hand and the gun in the other this he happily effected and escaped. (2:127–28)

The diaries recorded many encounters with Indians. Most of the Indians were peaceful but a dangerous situation occurred when Lewis and a small party from the expedition met a band of Blackfeet Indians. Lewis camped with the Indians, but he set a guard because he was afraid that they would attempt to steal his party's horses. In the early morning the guard "carelessly laid his gun down," and the Indians seized this chance to steal it and several others. One member of the expedition saw the theft and cried out, waking Lewis, who later reported the battle that ensued:

I jumped up and asked what was the matter which I quickly learned when I saw Drewyer in a scuffle with the indian for his gun. I reached to seize my gun but found her gone, I then drew a pistol from my holster and terning myself about saw the indian making off with my gun I ran at him with my pistol and bid him lay down my gun which he was in the act of doing when the Fieldses returned and drew up their guns to shoot him which I forbid as he did not appear to be about to make any resistance or commit any offensive act, he droped the gun and walked slowly off, I picked up her instantly, Drewyer having about this time recovered his gun and pouch asked me if he might not kill the fellow which I also forbid as the Indian did not appear to wish to kill us.

Then, as the Indians tried to drive off the party's horses, Lewis gave pursuit:

I called to them as I had done several times before and I would shoot them if they did not give me my horse and raised my gun, one of them jumped behind a rock and spoke to the other who turned around and stoped at the distance of 30 steps from me and I shot him through the belly, he fell to his knees and on his wright elbow from which position he partly raised himself up and fired at me, and turning himself about crawled in behind a rock which was a few feet from him. He overshot me, being bearheaded I felt the wind of his bullet very distinctly. (5:224–25)

Shortly after this narrow brush with death, Lewis rejoined his men and they rode off to join the rest of the expedition.

While Lewis and Clark do not seem to have been hostile to the Indians they met, they hardly pictured them as noble savages. Assuming the pose of scientific observers, they tried to be objective in recording the cultures of the various Indian nations, but their most vivid accounts were of incidents that showed the savagery forced on the Indian by his primitive way of life. In the following entry some Indians, starving from lack of game, devoured a deer shot by one of the men of the expedition:

Each one had a piece of some discription and all eating most ravenously. Some were eating the kidnies the melt and liver and blood running from the corners of their mouths, others were in a similar situation with the paunch and guts but the exuding substance in this case from their lips was of a different discription. One of the last who att[r]acted my attention particularly had been fortunate in his allotment or reather active in the division, he had provided himself with about nine feet of the small guts one end of which he was chewing on while with his hands he was squeezing the contents out at the other. I really did not untill now think that human nature ever presented itself in a shape so nearly allyed to the brute creation. I viewed these poor starved divils with pity and compassion. (2:355)

Even when they described Indian nations whose culture showed considerable complexity, Lewis and Clark presented themselves in their diaries as representatives of a paternalistic government whose "great father" would protect tribes that wisely accepted its benign control. The diarists never questioned the superiority of their culture over that of the Indians or doubted the eventual domination of their civilization over the Indians' wilderness.

This attitude was supported if not fostered by the specific instructions to the expedition. Jefferson had indicated that the expedition's purposes included the "extending and strengthening of the authority" of the United States (7:249), and even earlier (in 1803) Jefferson's secret message to Congress had stated the importance of encouraging the Indians to leave their nomadic life so that more land could be sold to white settlers (7:206). Given these instructions, it is clear that Lewis and Clark were aware that they were in the vanguard of cultural change. The modern reader can use a knowledge of history to see the expedition as the beginning of a period of expansion which in less than a century would see European people and their culture almost totally supplant the Indians and their way of life.

Lewis and Clark recorded surprisingly few direct statements in their diaries about the significance of their endeavor, but their descriptions and catalogs convey to their readers the impression that these diarists knew that the world they were recording would soon be profoundly altered, and that each specimen collected and each position recorded was a step toward such change. In this process the diary was as important an instrument as any that they carried.

Zebulon Pike (1779–1813)

In 1806, the same year that the Lewis and Clark expedition returned from its exploration of the Northwest, Zebulon Pike's party left St. Louis to explore the southern portion of the Louisiana Territory. The only dangers they expected were those of the wilderness, but by late September they learned that a large party of Spanish soldiers had been sent to intercept them and either turn them back or take them prisoner. Confident in his talents as a soldier and in the security of his position as an American exploring American property, Pike continued on.

Initially, the threat of the Spanish forces and other dangers remained unrealized, and the early diary centers around routine business. Occasionally in this portion of the diary Pike departed from a straightforward account and provided interesting descriptions of such diverse subjects as the exploration of a prairie dog town, an encounter with Indians who attempted to steal guns and other supplies, and his attempt to scale the peak now named for him. Such digressions weakened the unity of the diary, but they gave Pike opportunities to demonstrate his writing skill.

In December, Pike wrote movingly of the scarcity of game that resulted in short rations, and that, combined with the onset of bitter cold, made the party's situation dangerous:

Here I must take the liberty of observing that in this situation, the hardships and privations we underwent, were on this day brought more fully to our mind. Having been accustomed to some degree of relaxation, and extra enjoyments; but here 800 miles from the frontiers of our country, in the most inclement season of the year; not one person clothed for the winter, many without blankets, (having been obliged to cut them up for socks, &c.) and now laying down at night on snow or wet ground: one side burning whilst the other was pierced with the cold wind; this was in part the situation of the party whilst some were endeavoring to make a miserable substitute of raw buffalo hide for shoes &c. I will not speak of diet, as I conceive that to be beneath the serious consideration of a man on a voyage of such nature. We spent the day as agreeably as could be expected from men in our situation.[4]

These difficulties provide not only a dramatic subject, but a compelling theme to interconnect the incidents in the account. Pike tried to strike a balance between his desire to show the heroism of his men and his wish to assert their willingness to endure hardships.

Yet Pike convincingly shows that his party's sufferings went beyond those that might reasonably have been expected of them. Climbing steep slopes, surviving on berries and boiled deerskin, and suffering from frostbite, he and his followers almost lost hope. The entries for January 18 and 19, 1807, show the tenuousness of their survival and the strength and cohesiveness of their spirits:

18th January, Sunday.—We started two of the men least injured; (the doctor and myself, who fortunately were untouched by the frost) also went out to hunt something to preserve existence, near evening we wounded a buffalo with three balls, but had the mortification to see him run off notwithstanding. We concluded it was useless to go home to add to the general gloom, and went amongst some rocks where we encamped and sat up all night; from the intense cold it was impossible to sleep. Hungry and without cover.

19th January, Monday.—We again took the field and after crawling about one mile in the snow, got to shoot eight times among a gang of buffalo, and could plainly perceive two or three to be badly wounded, but by accident they took wind of us, and to our great mortification all were able to run off. By this time I had become extremely weak and faint, being the fourth day, since we had received substenance; all of which we were marching hard and the last night had scarcely closed our eyes to sleep. We were inclining our course to a point of woods determined to remain absent and die by ourselves rather than to return to our camp and behold the misery of our poor lads, when we discovered a gang of buffalo coming along at some distance. With great exertions I made out to run and place myself behind some cedars and by the greatest of good luck, the first shot stopped one, which we killed in three more shots; and by the dusk had cut each of us a heavy load with which we determined immediately to proceed to the camp in order to relieve the anxiety of our men, and carry the poor fellows some food. We arrived there about 12 o'clock, and when I threw my load down, it was with difficulty I prevented myself from falling; I was attacked with a giddiness of the head, which lasted for some minutes. On the countenances of the men was not a frown, nor a desponding eye; but all seemed happy to hail their officer and companions, yet not a mouthful had they eaten for four days. On demanding what was their thoughts, the sergeant replied, on the morrow the most robust had determined to set out in search of us; and not return unless they found us, or killed something to preserve the life of their starving companions. (369–70)

Pike demonstrated the way in which the bravery and effort of his party enabled it to overcome even such serious problems; his experiences recorded in the diary suggest that with such heroic efforts Americans might tame the wilderness. Indeed, by February Pike and his men had been able to improve their situation to the point where they could build a stockade as a defense against both the weather and human enemies.

Pike anticipated a conflict with the Spanish, but when the Spanish troops arrived, he found that he had strayed from his route and entered Spanish territory. Finding himself in the wrong, Pike agreed to accompany the Spaniards as their enforced guest. From this point he changed his diary's focus, taking on the diplomatic diarist's sense of being a representative of his society who, while possessing an overt freedom of action, recognizes that his freedom is circumscribed by his situation. This section of the diary is not unrelated to the wilderness experience. The same courage and effort that preserved Pike and his party in the wild, helped them to deal with the Spaniards. Moreover, Pike's account never ceased to display the crucial features of the exploration diary. Pike preserved his sense that the things he saw would allow him to reveal an unknown world to the readers of his own society.

In the Spanish territory Pike and his group were treated too graciously for enemies, too treacherously for friends. Typical of this section of the diary is the following excerpt recording Pike's reply to the accusations of a Spanish officer that Pike had been prompting a revolt by spreading political and religious opinions:

I replied that it was true I had held various and free conversations on the subjects complained of, but only with men high in office, who might be supposed to be firmly attached to the king, and partial to the government of their country. That I had never gone among the poor and illiterate, preaching up republicanism or a free government. That as to the catholic religion, I had only combatted some of what I conceived to be its illiberal dogmas; but that I had spoken of it in all instances as a respectable branch of the Christian religion, which as well as all others, was tolerated in the United States; but that, had I come to the kingdom on a diplomatic character, delicacy towards the government would have sealed my lips. Had I been a prisoner of war, personal safety might have had the same effect; but being there in the capacity which I was; not voluntarily, but by coercion of the Spanish government, but, who at the same time had officially notified me that they did not consider me under any restraint whatever—therefore, when called on, should always give my opinions freely, either as to politics or religion; but at the same time with urbanity, and a proper respect to the legitimate authorities of the country where I was.

He replied, "Well you may then rest assured your conduct will be represented in no very favorable point of view to your government."

I replied, "To my government I am certainly responsible and to no other." (419)

Pike's pride in being an American, which had been an animating force behind his efforts at exploration, now animated discussions with Spanish officials that were limited but never hidden by a diplomatic caution. He acted like the soldier he was, recognizing that his position was weak but maintaining his confident position as a camouflaging defense. Such blunt courage allows the reader to perceive as genuine the exuberance Pike displayed when, after the Spanish finally allowed him to return to his country, he first saw the American flag: "Language cannot express the gaiety of my heart when I once more beheld the standard of my country waved aloft! 'All hail,' cried I, 'the ever sacred name of country, in which is embraced that of kindred friends, and every other tie which is dear to the soul of man!'" (448–49). Such patriotism would be shared by his fellow Americans, who shortly after his return would print and read his account.

Henry Rowe Schoolcraft (1793–1864)

Schoolcraft wrote several diaries of his frontier explorations. The published portions describe trips to Missouri and Arkansas in 1818–19 and explorations in 1820–21 as a member of expeditions led by Governor Lewis Cass through Michigan, Minnesota, and Illinois. In the introduction to his *Narrative Journal of Travels,* Schoolcraft wrote that the scientific observations of his expedition had been made to satisfy the demands of a new "era . . . in the moral history" of America. His assumption was that his own culture would be changed and advanced by knowledge from the frontier.[5]

Like Lewis and Clark, Schoolcraft saw his explorations as important to the development of the American nation. An important theme of his journal was its author's participation in a large and "laudable" movement "in all parts of the union to explore the geography and call into action the hidden resources of the country" (6/16/20). Schoolcraft was trained as a geologist, and his early diaries were written about a trip to the Ozarks to view the lead mines and other sites of mineralogical interest. His descriptions, even those of "some of the most picturesque and sublime views," sometimes contain language about "calcareous rock" or "a substratum of very sterile gravelly alluvion." However, in most of his record Schoolcraft does not focus on scientific facts. For example, an early description of a huge cave culminated not in a scientific description but in a comment on the "wonder and awe" at such sights which produced "impressions in regard to our own origin, nature, and end, and the mysterious connection between the Creator of these stupendous works and ourselves, which many have before felt." Indeed, for Schoolcraft the end of such an experience was not the exaltation of rational inquiry, but the conclusion that "human reason has no clue by which the mystery may be solved" (11/12/18).

Such entries display an emotion and a tone foreign to the records of Lewis and Clark. When at one point members of the party were separated and feared lost in a "rugged" area, Schoolcraft wrote: "Night was rapidly closing around us, and after firing repeated signal guns, and sending out in all directions, nothing could be heard of them. The feelings of the party may be imagined upon this occasion, seated, as we were, in the midst of the most awful solitudes, and in a region which had impressed every individual with an indescribable feeling that was manifested in a general anxiety to depart from it" (6/28/20). It is not just expressions like "awful solitudes" that are significant here, but also the general attention to feeling over fact and the admission that there are some concerns that defy description or categorization.

In describing the frontier Schoolcraft painted a picture in keeping with some of the wild, romantic images that would become a standard part of American landscape painting in that and the following decades. Schoolcraft asserted that in such a place "one cannot help fancying that he has gone to the ends of the earth, and beyond the boundaries appointed for the residence of man." This region, bounded by "dark hemlock forests, and yawning gulfs more dreary and forbidding to the eye," even included those staples of romantic landscape painting, "the blasted trees, which either lie prostrate at the foot of the bluffs or hang in a threatening posture above" (6/28/20).

Some of these romanticized descriptions were added during the process of revision for publication. During this process Schoolcraft also inserted passages from the poems of Alexander Pope, Sir Walter Scott, Philip Freneau, and others. Such insertions all support a reader's perception that Schoolcraft saw his diary as having as great a relationship to literature as to science. In fact, Schoolcraft had early displayed an interest in literature. At fifteen he had published both poems and essays, and at sixteen had organized a local literary society.[6]

Schoolcraft also made frequent reference to the diaries, accounts, and other records of explorers like Pike, MacKenzie, and La Hontan, a technique that helped him to suggest that his work was part of a tradition. In using such sources Schoolcraft was not above quoting out of context so that the source better supported his argument. At one point he manipulated a quotation of the Baron de La Hontan so that it seemed that the baron was endorsing a statement that asserted the superiority of the Indian's social values over those of the Europeans. However, it was Schoolcraft, the nineteenth-century American, and not La Hontan, the eighteenth-century European, who wished to praise the Indian position that the only human distinctions should be those that result from individual talent and effort. La Hontan considered the Indians' claim that "a man is not a man with us any further than riches will make him so" an attempt to "pretend that their contented way of living surpasses" that of "the Europeans."[7]

Schoolcraft was not always drawn to the wonders of nature and the value of the primitive. In one early entry he wrote about the uneasy sleep in the wilderness of travelers who spent the night in "fear of the Indians on the one hand, and the approach of wild animals on the other" (11/9/18). In another passage he told how, after eating a "frugal meal of dried venison, bread and water," he and his companions "were almost imperceptibly drawn into a conversation on . . . [a] comparison between savage and civilized society." He then ended the entry with a poem he wrote on the walls of the cave in which they had eaten; a portion of it reads:

> Spirits of Caverns, goddess blest!
> Hear a suppliant's fond request,
> One, who nor a wanton calls
> Or intruder in thy walls;
> One who spills not on the plain
> Blood for sport or worldly gain,
> Like his red barbarian kin
> Deep in murder foul in sin;
> Or with high horrific yells
> Bends thy dark and silent cells;

(11/22/18)

This dark portrait of the nature and behavior of the Indians comes from an early entry, written when Schoolcraft had had only limited contact with them. Later, as he became more familiar with the Indian tribes, his portrait became steadily more positive. Part of this change may have resulted from his experiences with the whites he encountered on the frontier whose behavior suggested that savagery resulted from environment, not race. In one scene he told of being an "unwilling witness" to a drunken brawl among some hunter-traders:

Every mouth hand and foot were in motion. Some drank, some sang, some danced, a considerable portion attempted all three together, and a scene of undistinguishable brawling and riot ensued. An occasional quarrel gave variety to the scene, and now and then, one drunker than the rest, fell sprawling on the floor, and for a while remained quiet. We alone remained listeners to this exhibition of human noises, beastly intoxication, and mental and physical nastiness. (1/16/19)

Not only did these frontiersmen display all the animalistic behavior of savages, but they had brought the worst of civilization. Schoolcraft noted that "the love of gain" had already "found its way into these remote woods." Crossing "that boundary in our land, within which virtue prompts, wisdom teaches, and law restrains," he had not gotten "beyond the influence of money" (12/14/18). In a poem published with one of his diaries in 1820 Schoolcraft wrote of "the stream of migration that rolled to the west."

> They are driving the savage before them amain,
> And people each forest and culture each plain. . . .
> The exiles of Europe, the poor the oppress'd.
> All, all are bending their steps to the west.
> One object impells them, one passion inspires—
> The rage for improvement, for wealth the desires.

Schoolcraft saw that the western movement was inspired not only by a desire for greatness and the advance of culture but also for the "Increase of estate." In the poem this western invasion prompted "the king of minerals," a fictional ruler of rocks and metals who had lived in peace with the Indians, to plan a war against these new settlers whose "all conquering press" would plunder his domain.[8]

Not all of the Indians Schoolcraft encountered were friendly. One objective of the Cass expeditions was to arrange for the refortifying of garrisons which the French had constructed many years before to guard "the points commanding all the natural avenues and passes of the lakes" (6/16/20). A necessary step in accomplishing this task was occupying and fortifying land held by the Indians. At one point in the negotiations Schoolcraft's party had reason to fear an Indian attack. An Indian chief "drew his warlance and stuck it furiously in the ground before him, and assumed a look of savage wildness, which appeared to have a corresponding effect on the other Indians." However, while the party "stood prepared to encounter the shock" of an attack, the situation was resolved amicably through negotiation (6/26/20).

More often, Schoolcraft's description of the Indians emphasized their admirable traits. In one extended entry he related the story of a Chippewa band who, to repudiate an accusation that they had been less active in a current war than other bands of the tribe, attacked a Sioux camp holding ten times as many warriors as their own group and then retreated to make their final stand:

> To transmit the fame of this exploit to their nation, they had appointed the youngest warrior of their number to watch on an adjoining hill and when their fate was terminated, to carry the news to their friends. By this it seems that they had previously determined to die in their intrenchments. This messenger had not been long returned, when we reached Grand Island, where he sung the exploits of his departed friends. He was a tall and beautiful youth, with a manly countenance, expressive eyes, and formed with the most perfect symmetry,—and among all the tribes of Indians whom I have visited, I never felt, for any individual, such a mingled feeling of interest and admiration. (6/21/20)

Schoolcraft became fascinated with Indian culture and its stress on the advantages of "their mode of life" which favored "a healthful constitution of body." Similarly, he sought to squelch derogatory misconceptions about them, such as the belief that Indian mothers destroy their "ill formed children" (7/15/20). One exception to Schoolcraft's praise of the Indians was his condemnation of their treatment of their women, whom he found "doomed to drudgery and hardship from infancy." A husband might punish infidelity in a wife "with the loss of her hair, nose, and perhaps her life." Nor did this degradation end with death. Schoolcraft wrote that "if a warrior dies, his war club and other weapons and ornaments, are buried with him, as it is supposed, he will require them in another world. If it is a woman that dies, a paddle and carrying strap are buried with her that she may perform the same drudgery in a future state as she is required to do in this" (7/15/20).

Schoolcraft's interest in the American Indian continued long after the period in which he wrote his most famous exploration diaries. In 1821, after the conclusion of the Cass expedition, he first accepted the post of secretary to the United States Indian treaty commissioners, and in 1822 he became the Indian agent for the Upper Great Lakes. In the latter position Schoolcraft had an excellent opportunity to study Indian culture. Among his contributions to our knowledge of the Indians were portions of dictionaries and grammars of the Indian languages and "what was probably the first 'oral history' program in America." Schoolcraft collected Indian "lodge stories"; among the legends he recorded was one that became the source for Longfellow's *Hiawatha*.[9]

John Charles Frémont (1813–1890)

Frémont's fame came as the result of the publication of his exploration diaries, covering the first two of his five expeditions. From May 22 until October 17, 1842, Frémont followed a route from St. Louis, Missouri, to the continental divide in western Wyoming, which approximated a portion of what would come to be called the Oregon Trail. His second expedition began on May 17, 1843, and started on a more southerly route through Kansas and Colorado. Frémont turned northward to Oregon, arriving at Fort Vancouver in November, and then went south into California before returning on August 6, 1844.[10]

Like Schoolcraft's diary, John Charles Frémont's personal record emphasized the heroism, beauty, and excitement of explorations in the western wilderness by using language that reflects its author's interest in literature and his romantic view of history. For Frémont, "Indians and Buffalo make the poetry . . . of the prairie," and their effect on both the diarist and his diary is one of "exhilaration."[11] He made a buffalo hunt into a heroic battle in which Kit Carson (whose place as a folk hero was established by Frémont's work) seems a modern knight bravely pursuing monsters. In one passage Frémont even ennobled his own mount:

My Horse was a trained hunter, famous in the west under the name of Proveau, and with his eyes flashing and the foam flying from his mouth, [he] sprang on after the cow like a tiger. In a few moments he brought me alongside of her, and rising in the stirrups, I fired at the distance of a yard, the ball entering the termination of the long hair, and passing near the heart. She fell headlong at the report of my gun. (1:187)

Through entries such as these Frémont made his experiences seem particularly exciting. He managed to convey a sense of adventure and heroic achievement even though he and his party traveled through better-known territory than did Lewis and Clark and faced fewer dangers and hardships than Pike and his companions. Not all of Frémont's explorations were free from difficulty; in one arduous winter crossing of the Sierra Nevada Mountains he and his companions were reduced to killing their dogs and mules for food, but in general they experienced few serious problems (1:626-35).

Frémont's "poetry of the prairie" had its cruder side, and the source of this crudity was not always the hardships of the frontier. In one series of entries he wrote of his party's meeting with a Mexican whose horses had been stolen by a band of Indians. Volunteering to help in the recovery of these horses, Kit Carson and another of Frémont's men, Alexander Godey, rode off, to return the following day sounding "a war-whoop . . . such as Indians make when returning from a victorious enterprise." They had not only secured the stolen horses, but also "two bloody scalps, dangling from Godey's gun [which] announced that they had overtaken the Indians as well as the horses." The two men had pursued the Indians to their camp and attacked; and "the scalps of the fallen," one of whom proved to have been still alive, were "instantly stripped off" within view of an "old squaw, possibly his mother." Frémont explained that "the stout hearts" of Carson and Godey were so "appalled" by the "frightful spectacle" that "they did what humanity required, and quickly terminated the agonies of the gory savage." This description of the explorers' descent into the "heart of darkness" of the American wilderness should make one doubt if Frémont, who claimed that Carson and Godey were noble for having risked their lives for the property of strangers, knew the meaning of the words *humanity* and *savage* (1:681). Preuss, describing the same incident in his diary, showed that not all of Frémont's men took his view of this massacre, and that Frémont was inclined to select details that confirmed his own bias:

Are not these whites much worse than the Indians? The more noble Indians take from the killed enemy only a piece of the scalp, somewhat as large as the tonsure of a priest. These two heroes, who shot the Indians creeping up on them from behind, brought along the entire scalp. The Indians are braver in a similar situation. Before they shoot they raise a yelling war whoop. Kit and Alex sneaked like cats, as close as possible. Kit shot an Indian in the back. . . . To me such butchery is disgusting, but Frémont is in high spirits. I believe he would exchange all observations for a scalp taken by his own hand.[12]

Even when there was no imminent threat, Frémont would set his scene to create an atmosphere of tension. In one entry in which he described his ascent of "Snow Peak"[13] Frémont emphasized his own courage by reminding his readers that he had been ill only the day before and heightened the sense of danger by explaining that the climb was so difficult that he found it necessary to switch to thin-soled moccasins "as now the use of our toes became necessary to a further advance." Furthermore, in describing the top of the mountain, he repeatedly noted how precarious that summit was, writing that "it seemed a breath would have hurled [it] into the abyss below," and that "another step would have precipitated me into an immense snow field five hundred feet below." Even a bumblebee encountered at the summit is transmuted into a Romantic symbol of heroic exploration: "It was a strange place, the icy rock and the highest peak of the Rocky Mountains, for a lover of warm sunshine and flowers, and we pleased ourselves that he was the first of his species to cross the mountain barrier, a solitary pioneer to foretell the advance of civilization" (1:269–70).

Occasionally Frémont would resolve the tension he had created by providing some comic relief. In the excerpt just cited his party did not allow the exploring bumblebee "to continue his way unharmed, but . . . carried out the law of this country, where all animated nature seems at war; and seizing him immediately, put him in at least a fit place, in the leaves of a large book, among the flowers we had collected on our way" (1:270).

In another example of tension followed by comic relief Frémont used a storm to suggest danger: "A heavy bank of black clouds in the west came on us in a storm between nine and ten, preceded by a violent wind. The rain fell in such torrents that it was difficult to breathe facing the wind, the thunder rolled incessantly, and the whole sky was tremulous with lightning; now and then illuminated by a blinding flash succeeded by pitchy darkness." Frémont then used this setting as a background against which he could alternate real and imagined fears: a "badly chosen [camp site], surrounded on all sides by timbered hollows" that could hide an attack, and stories told around the campfire "of desperate and bloody Indian fights." It is, therefore, not surprising that when Kit Carson bravely galloped off to check on one man's excited cries that there twenty-seven Indians nearby, he returned to report that "the Indian war party of twenty-seven consisted of six elk" (1:179–80). Through entries such as these Frémont created an exciting diary. Thoreau in his essay "Walking" (1862) would assert that the "heroic age" was not dead, but only transported to the American West. Frémont's diary made the same assertion two decades earlier.

Although given to a Romantic view of his own actions, Frémont was not immediately won over by nature. Only gradually did he yield to his own sense of wonder. In his first description of the Wind River Mountains, he compared them unfavorably to the Alps:

As we passed over a slight rise near the river, we caught the first view of the Wind River mountains, appearing at this distance of about seventy miles, to be a low and dark mountainous ridge. The view dissipated in a moment the pictures which had been created in our minds, by many descriptions of travelers, who have compared these mountains to the Alps in Switzerland; and speak of the glittering peaks which rise in icy majesty amidst eternal glaciers nine or ten thousand feet into the region of eternal snows. (1:249–50)

However, a week later in a description of a mountain sunrise, Frémont's sense of the inferiority of the American landscape had already begun to moderate:

The scenery becomes hourly more interesting and grand, and the view here is truly magnificent; but, indeed, it needs something to repay the long prairie journey of a thousand miles. The sun had just shot above the wall and makes a magical change. The whole valley is glowing and bright and all the mountain peaks are gleaming like silver. Though these snow mountains are not the Alps, they have their own character of grandeur and magnificence, and will doubtless find pens and pencils to do them justice. (1:255)

Only a few days later the very notion of a hierarchical comparison had given way to a recognition of different but equal qualities:

Immediately at our feet a precipitous descent led to a confusion of defiles, and before him rose the mountains. . . . It is not by the splendor of far-off views, which have lent such a glory to the Alps, that these impress the mind; but by a giant disorder of enormous masses, and a savage sublimity of naked rock, in wonderful contrast with innumerable green spots of a rich floral beauty, shut up in their stern recesses. (1:262)

Frémont's language altered with his changing appreciation of the scenery. Simple descriptions became enriched by figurative language, poetic cadences, and alliterative effects until he was writing lines such as "Even to our great height the roar of the cataracts came up, and we could see them leaping down in lines of snowy foam" (1:260-61), and "We had accomplished an object of laudable ambition, and beyond the strict order of our instructions. We had climbed the loftiest peak of the rocky mountains, and looked down upon the snow a thousand feet below, and, standing where never human foot had stood before, felt the exultation of first explorers" (1:272).

Although to a modern reader such passages may seem too florid and self-congratulatory for a refined literary taste, they had the effect on their initial audience that Frémont desired. Appearing in print at a time when Americans were enthusiastic about westward expansion, they helped to make Frémont seem the hero they wished for.

Domestic and Foreign Travel Diaries

Americans have always seemed particularly interested in travel. While the novelty of the frontier was and continues to be a subject of great interest to American society, Americans have long recognized that regions already explored might not only prove interesting, but also offer opportunities for valuable discoveries. Among the reasons for this special interest may be the initial travel necessary for the immigrants who helped form American society to reach our shores; another may be the size and diversity of the nation itself. Even in this age of jet planes most Americans, including many of those who have taken vacations to distant lands, have seen little of their own country.

In the early nineteenth century Americans began to travel extensively. The Revolution ended the British prohibition on emigration beyond the Alleghenies and led to settlements in Tennessee, Kentucky, Ohio and elsewhere. Margaret Dwight Bell's diary is only one of the numerous diaries written by those early settlers. Soon explorations like those discussed earlier in this chapter opened the rest of the Northwest, Louisiana, and Oregon territories to both settlers and other travelers. Among these Parkman's journal of the Oregon Trail is an important example.

Of course, Americans continued to travel eastward to Europe. Some, such as Washington Irving, continued the British tradition of the European tour as an almost essential component of a young gentleman's education. Other diarists made their first trips abroad on business, as members of diplomatic missions, or in the company of diplomats or business travelers (we shall examine those of James Gallatin and John Quincy Adams in subsequent chapters). Many diarists declared their records to have been invaluable both in preserving and in organizing their experiences. A very common sentiment in such works is that these long-known countries offered unexpected wonders.

Margaret Van Horn Dwight Bell (1790–1834)

When Margaret Van Horn Dwight[14] began her trip from Connecticut to Ohio she also began an epistolary diary of her travels to be sent to her cousin Elizabeth Woolsey. Though on the last page of the work she instructed Elizabeth, "let no one see this but your own family," the several printings since its first publication in 1912 indicate that her diary attracted a wider readership than she could ever have anticipated.[15]

Three principle subjects are interwoven in the diary. The two most frequent of these are the difficulty of the journey itself and the coarse appearance and behavior of most of the people she encountered. The third subject, less frequently articulated but significantly related to the other two, is her concern about marriage. This concern is understandable in light of her situation. In 1810 few women could find alternatives to marriage because most careers were closed to them. Miss Dwight's situation was further proscribed by the conflicting elements that affected her status. She was well educated and from a cultured and socially prominent family, but she lacked wealth. These factors made her less suited for and probably less willing to take a menial occupation; at the same time, they limited her opportunities for a congenial marriage. Since she was twenty when she began her journey and since she expected to stay in Ohio for three years, one can understand one landlady's expectation that if Miss Dwight returned she "should never come back alone," but that she "would certainly be married in a little while" (6-7). However, the diarist's response was, "I am now more than ever determined not to oblige myself to spend my days there, by marrying should I even have the opportunity" (7).

Miss Dwight's unwillingness to settle permanently in the West was the result of her pride, which, she declared, made her reluctant to be seen traveling by wagon and staying in crude accommodations. Even before she had gotten far west she found occasion to write:

I never will go to New Connecticut with a *Deacon* again, for we put up at every byeplace in the country to *save expence*—It is very grating to my pride to go into a tavern & furnish & cook my own provision—to ride in a wagon &c &c—but that I can possibly get along with—but to be oblig'd to pass the night in such a place as we are now in, just because it is a little cheaper, is more than I am willing to do—I should even rather drink clear rum out of the wooden bottle after the deacon has drank & wip'd it over with his hand, than to stay here another night—The house is very small & very dirty—it serves for a tavern, a store, & I should imagine hog's pen stable & every thing else—The air is so impure I have scarcely been able to swallow since I enter'd the house—The landlady is a fat, dirty, ugly looking creature, yet I must confess very obliging—She has a very suspicious countenance & I am very afraid of her—She seems to be master, as well as mistress & storekeeper, & from the great noise she has been making directly under me this half hour, I suspect she has been "stoning the raisins & watering the rum." (5)

Such descriptions of tavern life show it to have been as bad or worse than that about which Madam Knight complained in her diary a century earlier.

Miss Dwight's expectations of life in the more newly settled areas were continually being lowered as the journey proceeded. At one place she encountered women whom she called "*amazoons*—for they swore and flew about 'like *witches*' and talked and laugh'd about their sparks &c &c till it made us laugh so as almost to affront them" (14). On the other hand, she found herself perceived as an oddity because of her own manners and appearance, and she concluded in one instance that people had come "to see us *Yankees* as they would a learned pig" (16).

She was not frightened by the expectation that there might be "wild Indians" in Ohio, but she was terrified by the men drinking and gambling in the taverns where she was forced to stay. She wrote, "I was very much frighten'd by a drunken waggoner, who came up to me as I stood by the door waiting for a candle, he put his arm around my neck, & said something which I was too frighten'd to hear—"(36). Though she tried to make her fears seem less by writing that she rarely was so "insulted," her fears were based on real concerns. In the following excerpt, she told how a strange man entered her bedchamber:

I took off my frock & boots, & had scarcely lain down, when one of the wretches came into my room & lay down by me on the outside of the bed—I was frighten'd almost to death & clung to Mrs. Jackson who did not appear to mind it—& I lay for a quarter of an hour crying, & scolding & trembling, begging of him to leave me—At last, when persuaded I was in earnest, he begg'd of me not to take it amiss, as he intended no harm & only wish'd to become acquainted with me—A good for nothing brute, I wonder what he suppos'd I was—I don't know of any thought word or action of mine that could give him reason to suppose I would authorise such abominable insolence— (40)

That Miss Dwight escaped without harm was not sufficient to make her feel at ease. Nevertheless, as her following comment shows, she did try to respond to some situations with humor: "One waggoner very civilly offer'd to take Susan or me, on to Pitts[bur]g in his waggon if we were not like to get there till spring—It is not yet determin'd which shall go with him—" (36).

Despite such attempts at humor, as in the case of the following potential proposal, her humor frequently betrayed her great anxiety about her situation:

—I have the greater part of the time till now, felt in better spirits than I expected—my journal has been of use to me in that respect—I did not know but I should meet with the same fate that a cousin of Mr. Hall's did, who like me, was journeying to a new, if not a western country—She was married on her way & prevented from proceeding to her journey's end—There was a man today in Camptown where we stopt to eat, not oats but gingerbread, who enquired, or rather *expected* we were going to the Hio—we told him yes & he at once concluded it was to get husbands—He said winter was coming on & he wanted a wife & believ'd he must go there to get him one—I concluded of course the next thing would be, a proposal to Miss W. or me to stay behind to save trouble for us both; but nothing would suit him but a rich widow, so our hopes were soon at an end—Disappointment is the lot of man & we may as well bear them with a good grace—this thought restrain'd my tears at that time, but has not been able to since—What shall I do? (10–11)

Of course, her complaints in this excerpt were written in jest, but there was some serious concern behind them. This entry is only one of a number in which Dwight revealed that she had become less secure in her determination not to seek marriage at any cost. In another, she joked about having been "jolted" from her "high notions" so that she might be willing in her expectations of a husband "to descend from a judge to a blacksmith"; however, she could do so only while she was willing to risk remaining single. Eventually the words "get married,— get a husband" seemed "terrible" (29).

Dwight's revelations about her personal anxieties help the reader to discover a pattern in the diary that fits the experience of many Americans who migrated west in the nineteenth century. While some pioneers broke all connections with their past lives prior to going west, others brought the expectations and standards of their past with them. Some, like Dwight, expected that their stay would be temporary; but for most, the real West affected and changed their values in ways that they could not have anticipated. For Dwight these changes were significant. Her surprise at finding some intelligent wagoners in Pennsylvania and a pleasant town waiting for her in Ohio was in part a sign of her changing values. It is not that Dwight learned to accept crudity, but that she learned that the primitive simplicity of the western pioneers might be preferable to the coarse behavior practiced behind the veneer of manners in the "civilized" East.

The revelation by the editor of the diary that Miss Dwight became Mrs. Bell only a year after arriving in Ohio need not be taken as an indication that Dwight deserted her principles or standards. Rather, we may hope that her experience in traveling enabled her to refine her values. Miss Dwight became a member of American frontier society in part through the experiences described in her diary. By recording her personal situation she captured a moment in time and made her future readers understand more about the western migration than they might from novels and histories.

Francis Parkman (1823–1893)

Francis Parkman kept a number of interesting travel diaries. The earliest of the extant volumes covering travels in New Hampshire and Maine was written in the summer vacation of his freshman year at Harvard (1840) when Parkman was only seventeen. However, even the first entries are so regular and well developed that it seems likely that Parkman had had earlier experience with the form. One of the objects of the trip covered by this diary was "to have a taste of the half savage-like kind of life . . . and to see the wilderness where it was as yet uninvaded by the hand of man."[16] The diary has vivid accounts of his adventures, including difficult passages through the forests and dangerous climbs on the mountains. Nature was not merely a setting, but

a major and active character in the diary. Even the immovable mountains seemed to move; the peaks "rising . . . like the black waves of
the sea," the mists rolling down their sides, quivering a moment before
they "boiled up through the ravines and gorges" (15).

The next summer, Parkman kept a similar diary covering another
trip that included northwestern New York State as well as parts of New
England. A diary kept in the summer of 1843 is briefer than the earlier
two, but it is important in giving a glimpse of Parkman's early interest
in the historical research that would become his profession. At the end
of 1843 he sailed to Europe for a "grand tour," and again he began a
travel diary.

Only a few days into this diary Parkman began a series of fine
sketches of the sailors and passengers on his ship, showing his talent
for characterization. In one passage, for example, he recorded the talk
of a man who had once been on an expedition to the Oregon Territory
and was now the second mate on the ship:

"I've lost all my appetite and got a horse's! Here, steward. . . . What do [you]
call this here? Well never mind what it be; it goes down well anyhow." Here
he sat stuffing a minute or two in silence with his grisly whiskers close to the
table, rolling his eyes, and puffing out his ruddy cheeks. . . . "I've knowed
the time when I could have ate a Blackfoot Indian, bones and all, and couldn't
get a mouthful. . . . Some folks are always running after the doctor, and
getting sick. Eat—that's the way I do." (1:110–11)

Such characters form an important part of this diary, for Parkman delighted in the "infinite . . . diversity of human character" (2:411).
And while he did record a vivid account of the scenery and other attractions in Europe, he seems to have been writing an adventure rather
than a tour guide.

The reader comes to feel for the life and the people Parkman observed as well as for Parkman's youthful exuberance. Arriving at Gi-
braltar, shortly before the gates were about to close and without a
permit, he paid ferrymen to attempt what he had been told would be
a fruitless effort to get there in time. Going to Virgil's tomb, he had
to be restrained by his guides from swinging over a two-hundred-foot
drop in quest of a souvenir (1:118–19, 166–67). In Rome he gained
entrance to a monastery only to find that the monks thought he had
come "to profit from holy seclusion." Instead of leaving, he responded,
"Here is an adventure!" and seized the opportunity to explore something new (1:190–95).

By far the most important of Parkman's travel diaries is the one he kept from March 29 to October 1, 1846, which became the basis for his first and most famous book, *The Oregon Trail*. Parkman went on this western tour to gain information, especially about the ways of Indians, that might prove useful in the historical writing he was planning. He had other motives as well.[17] He was driven by a passion for the wild and the unknown, which he had demonstrated in his earlier diaries, and by a desire to overcome a number of ailments that had begun to plague him and that would continue for the rest of his life.

Traveling with only a few companions through dangerous country, Parkman risked a great deal; yet he was fortunate enough not only to avoid harm, but also to have a wide variety of experiences. He traveled through a great stretch of the American West, encountering many of the most interesting individuals of the period and members of a large number of different Indian tribes.

In the Oregon Trail journal Parkman continued to develop his skill in describing scenery. He could capture for his readers a "muddy creek . . . all teeming with life, animal and vegetable, just awakening in the warm sunshine," a "luxuriant wood . . . interlaced with vines like snakes, and all bursting into leaf and flower," or a "prairie scorched and arid—broken with vile ravines and buttes" (2:412, 454).

Good as his descriptions of the land were, Parkman's studies of people were even better. He saw human nature as greatly determined by the environment. When he encountered a stage driver who was so "bluff, boisterous, profane and coarse" that he fit Parkman's "idea of an Indian trader," the diarist was tempted to wonder whether this creature "could belong to the same species" as some of the refined women of his acquaintance. However, Parkman rejected the notion that the savage might seem to have a different inner nature from the civilized man. Instead, he concluded that the "essential distinctions" might be attributable to education, to experience. True, "a Wordsworth" or any man of high education might have little "in common with the brutish clods who were . . . [his] fellow passengers across the Alleghenies," but the brutishness of the stage driver need not be ascribed to some innate deficiency (2:408). The outer calm of the Indian warrior might "in part arise from temperament"; however, it could also result from "long training" (2:405).

Parkman realized that not all the traits prompted by the frontier were negative. He appears to have been pleased to note that "the western character" showed no trace of the "offishness" or the "contracted, reserved manner" that he detected in the English and Yankees (2:410–

11). He might condemn the thoughtlessness and argumentativeness and recklessness that doomed so many of those who attempted to cross the wilderness (Parkman actually encountered the Donner party on his travels); yet at the same time he could stand in awe at the courage that permitted old men, pretty girls with parasols, and families with wagonloads of children to make such long and hazardous journeys. [18]

Parkman was adept at capturing the color and excitement of Indian life, as in the following excerpt depicting a group of Indians crossing a ford to set up a new camp:

Men and boys, naked and dashing eagerly through the water—horses with lodge poles dragging through squaws and children, and sometimes a litter of puppies—gaily attired squaws, leading the horses of their lords—dogs with their burdens attached swimming among the horses and mules—dogs barking, horses breaking loose, children shouting—squaws thrusting into the ground the lance and shield of the master of the lodge—naked and splendidly formed men passing and repassing through the swift water. (2:441)

Mason Wade, editor of the *Journals,* juxtaposed the above passage with its revision in *The Oregon Trail* to show how the "sharpness of impression" of the former was sometimes lost through the "romanticization" and the addition of details in the latter (2:389). For example, "squaws" become "buxom young squaws, blooming in all the charms of vermilion" (2:389–90). The revised versions of such scenes in *The Oregon Trail* are usually smoother but often less vital than those in the originals, not only because of such stretching and romanticization, but also because the energy of such nonstandard usage as dashes and incomplete sentences was edited out. These changes are all the more to be regretted as Parkman, the diarist, had achieved that delicate balance between the distracting omission of language that can weaken some otherwise fine diaries and the self-consciously flowery style that mars others. When we read in Parkman's diary that the "domestic implements" of some immigrants "had an old fashioned air: chairs of ash-silvers—gourd dippers—kettles—anvil—bellows—old bureaus—clothing—bedding—frying pans," we are not likely to be dissatisfied that we don't know the color of the dippers or the number of drawers in each bureau (2:410).

The diary shows that Parkman succeeded in his desire to learn about the Indian tribes of the American West. One of his most interesting observations involves the relationship between possessions and behavior among the Sioux he encountered. This relationship may have been particularly interesting for Parkman because it was so alien to his own culture, rooted as it was in the Protestant ethic that connected a man's personal and economic worth yet considered overt attempts at economic gain as unworthy. Parkman registered surprise at the covetousness of the Sioux, declaring that their worst trait was that "their appetites for presents [was] insatiable—the more that is given to them the more they expect." Parkman expressed his amazement at finding that "at meals, no matter how slender the repast may be, chiefs warriors surround us with eager eyes to wait for a portion, and this although their bellies may be full to bursting. . . . They will come a two days' journey for the sake of your cup of coffee" (2:453). Parkman used his observations well, concluding that behavior in what seemed an insignificant activity might be a key to the Sioux character.

Parkman kept a number of other personal records, usually during periods of travel, at intervals throughout the rest of his life. However, these notebooks contain only few, usually fragmentary, entries. The best of Parkman's diaries are those of his youth.

Washington Irving (1783–1859)

From his earliest diary, an account of a trip in New York State written in 1803, until his last European trip in 1846, Washington Irving kept a series of interesting and extensive personal records. These records can be divided into two types: true diary sections composed of regular dated entries and notebook sections with a variety of (generally undated) materials. Irving occasionally alternated between the two forms in the same manuscript book, but they are more often separate. Indeed, Irving more usually used different types of writing materials.[19]

The notebook sections include extracts copied from books that Irving had read as well as original observations by him. Some of these original notes are similar to materials in the true diary sections, but more fragmentary both in their internal syntax and in their external context. A number of them are presented as "views" almost in the way that a tourist today might make a notation on the margin of a photograph: "View from Stirling castle at Sunset—clouds & mist shrouding some part of the prospect—splendid effect of sun darting her rays into the mist," or "Kenmore—beautiful view <of the> Loch Tay from the road."[20] Lacking a camera, Irving sometimes accompanied such notes with a sketch, but more often, as in the following passage, his words provided the picture:

Mingled masses of Wood & Grey rock—rich green of the mountain gullies where the torrents occasionally deposit soil & impart moisture. <Broad> The Idea of a broad & at the same time deep & unobstructed view of the river fills the mind—Possesses Sublimity. . . . Mountain brook splashing & dashing along among mossy rocks—trees half fallen whose foliage overhang the water & seem dripping with humidity—weeds & nameless vagrant vines hanging in festoons—crumbling moisture of the soil—old trunks of trees mouldering . . . dewy coldness of the mountain rifts thro which the water runs. (2:31)

This Catskill mountain scene, like many others in the journals, reveals Irving's affinity with the painters of the Hudson River School.[21]

A large number of the notes contain ideas for or drafts of parts of Irving's fiction and essays. In his "Notebook of 1810," for example, he preserved his impression of an "Old Maid sarcastic & severe[,] the spirit of youth evaporated—like pipe of wine when the spirit has been drawn off [—] what remains turns to vinegar." This material seems to have been the source of the following passage from *Bracebridge Hall* describing "Mrs. Hannah, a prim, pragmatical old maid. . . . she has kept her virtue by her until it has turned sour, and now every word and look smacks of verjuice" (2:30, 2:30n).

The bulk of Irving's journalizing, especially that portion most relevant for consideration as literature, consists of travel diaries. Many of these became useful as the basis for some of his other literary works, but they should not really be classed as literary notebooks because, with the possible exception of his diary of his western tour, their use for other writing seems secondary. This interpretation of Irving's intentions in this regard seems supported by the fact that Irving would terminate these diaries when he returned home from his travels even though his attention to details useful in his writing hardly ceased at those points.

Irving's longest periods of journalizing covered travels in Europe, one during the period from 1804 to 1806 and another from 1815 to 1832.[22] The early entries in the diary of the first trip abroad show Irving's eye for details, such as the type of stone used in the buildings, the width of the alleys, the making of ravioli. His taste was for romantic images, such as "cottages embowered in groves of elms and their white washed walls over run with vines," which called to mind "those retreats of rural happiness so often sung by our pastoral poets" (1:33), or a road that offered "a succession of wild & romantic mountain scenery with now and then a view of a distant valley all rendered

more charming by the enlivening aid of a . . . delightful morning"
(1:91).

However, Irving's attention was drawn most strongly by the people,
especially when their behavior contrasted with that which he had observed in America:

It amuses me very much to walk the streets and observe the many ways these
people have of getting a living of which we have no idea in America. The
fruit women divert me the most, to see them with their old fashioned long
wasted [*sic*] dresses their arms stuck akimbo . . . monstrous caps on their
heads surmounted with a huge basket of fruit, thus decked off they straddle
along the pavement bawling out their merchandise in a voice every tone of
which is as sharp as vinegar. (1:38)

Irving's diary is full of unusual events, such as a balloon ascension,
an attack at sea by a privateer, and the execution of a romantically
heroic brigand known as the "great devil." It also contains many amus-
ing anecdotes. In one, Irving accompanied an American captain into a
store that sold musical instruments. The captain had decided not to
buy anything, but, fascinated by the "pretty little black eyed woman"
who kept the shop, he turned to Irving "& whispered with a knowing
wink 'Dam'me lets go and over haul her trumpery, you'l see how she'll
try to come along side of us, but the devil a sous do I lay out for her
fiddles and music mills.'" However, as Irving showed, the captain was
not so clever as he thought himself. "By the help of music & wine and
flattery & a pretty face the honest captain was so bewildered that before
he got out of the ware room he had bought a large hand organ for 400
livres (a third more than it was worth) which he did not know what
the devil to do with after he had got it" (1:46).

For Irving, a true Romantic, every scene brought with it thoughts
of magic, mystery, or ancient glory, and every thought carried with it
echoes of literature. But Irving, the true diarist, did not overlook reality. Indeed, the contrast between his concrete observations and his imaginative visions provides a tension that produced his particular
perceptions. In the following excerpts from one telling entry recounting a distant view of the city of Naples, we can observe the pattern of
Irving's vision:

There is no country where the prospects so much interest my mind and awaken
such a variety of ideas as in Italy. Every mountain—every valley every plain

tells some striking history. On casting my eyes around some majestic ruin carries my fancy back to the ages of Roman splendor. . . . Some sepu[l]chral monument awakens in my mind the recollections of a man famous for his virtues or detestable for his vices—in the midst of these reflections an old castle frowning on the brow of an eminence transports my imagination to the latter days of chivalry & romance. I picture myself issuing from the gateway the gallant knight . . . I see the hospitable feast, the tilt, the tournament and every other custom that distinguishes that enthusiastic age when prowess was the effect of love and when gallantry & romance presided over every transaction. From these pleasing reveries my mind is recalled to the contemplation of present circumstances & objects. I behold misery indolence & ignorance at every turn—He sees a perfect Canaan around him and inhabitants starving in the midst of it. The land scarcely cultivated—The peasant tills it with a heavy brow satisfied if he can snatch from it a scanty subsistence. Such are the baneful effects of despotic governments—of priest craft & superstition—of personal oppression and Slavery of thought. (1:257–58)

His portrait of Rome follows the same pattern as this reverie on Naples. On seeing Rome from a distant hilltop, Irving first remarked on the "melancholy yet pleasing sensations" produced by a view of the Tiber rolling "its yellow turbid stream" and "the church of St. Peters . . . that magnificent Edifice"; then went on at length to contrast ancient Rome, which "gave laws to nations and proudly assumed the title of '*Mistress of the World*,'" with its present "state of ignorance & poverty." Again Irving's villains were the nobility and the priests, who he felt had maintained their power by keeping the people "servile and superstitious" (1:277–78).

The "power of Fancy," the creative force of the imagination, turned Irving's mind toward an earlier age, which had what seemed a loftier and more exciting set of circumstances and values, and away from the miseries he saw around him. These romantic fantasies called forth images from literature, history, and folklore, while his origins in republican and mostly Protestant America provided the values that shaped his analysis, sometimes making his statements more extreme than his objective perceptions seem to have supported.

Certainly Irving experienced things in Italy that were worthy of objection. He saw ancient monuments whose very stones had been looted "to form several palaces and churches" (1:264–65) and streets crowded with beggars and pimps; he endured attempted extortions and other "impositions of innkeepers servants &c—from wretched carriages, roguish drivers, corrupt customs house officers," and numerous others who "never fail to take advantages of strangers that do not speak their language" (1:315, 321). However, he also encountered kindness, innocence, and sensitivity.

Of course, Irving was not alone in favoring his native land. In one entry he told of a Swiss waiter who disbelieved the favorable reports he had heard of America because he was convinced that, seeking to attract people to fight in wars against the Indians, the American government suppressed any letters or other communications about the true situation in the United States (1:404–5).

Toward the beginning of his first European trip Irving wrote in his diary, "Amid all the scenes of novelty and pleasure that surround me, I assure you my thoughts often return to <home> . . . [and] throws a damp over my spirits which I find it difficult to shake off. This however I hope will wear away in time as I become more a 'Citizen of the World'" (1:39). When he returned to New York in 1806 he was still very much the youthful American, but during his long residence in Europe from 1815 to 1832 he indeed became a "Citizen of the World" as well as the first American fiction writer to have a significant reputation on both sides of the Atlantic.

The diary of his later European residence is much inferior to the earlier one. It contains bits of highly interesting material and occasionally longer and more complete entries, such as a series of drafts for a story about a phantom army in Austria. However, most of the entries in the later diary are not only briefer than those in the early record, but also largely composed of incomplete sentences separated by dashes. The diaries written from 1804 to 1805 are stronger in both style and content.

In 1832 Irving went west at the invitation of Judge Ellsworth, one of the commissioners charged with the removal of several Indian tribes to lands further west. In his diary of this western tour Irving continued the practice from his later European diaries of writing fragmentary sentences. But, as in the following excerpt, that style frequently created poetic cadences in the western tour diary that are not present in the European diaries:

Road winds by deep brook—a link of clear pools—fine views from the height of distant prairies, and of hills beyond the Arkansas—golden day—pure and delightful air. After much tortuous march and climbing hills, threading narrow but romantic valleys we come upon the Arkansas—broad sandy shore—forests—elk deer—buffalo—opossum—turkeys—banks of cotton trees and willow. Picturesque look of troops straggling along the shore—some in groups among the willows—turn in thro' thick bushes tangled with grape and pea vines. (*T*,3:144)

Irving's travel experience also served to focus and to unify the content in a way that makes the western diary a better literary work. Moreover, in moving from the civility of European society to the wilderness, Irving at the age of forty-nine seems to have recaptured some of the adventurous spirit of his early diaries. Again he faced unknown dangers, and though he was traveling through midwestern prairie rather than Alpine passes and encountering Indian bands rather than privateers or Italian brigands, he was still experiencing scenery and events that inspired his romantic imagination.

Irving was still discovering the stuff of folklore and legend. For example, he recorded a tale that, if set in some German town, would immediately be recognized as an example of the Gothic. In the story a young Indian who returns to his camp finds all of his people gone except his fiancée:

"Where is the camp?" "It is struck. They are gone to such a place." "And what are you doing here?" "Waiting for you." He gave her his bundle and walked ahead according to the Indian custom—approaching the camp the girl sat down at the foot of a tree and said, "I will wait here. It is not proper for us to return together." He entered the town—told his sister to go after the girl—she is dead—died a few days since. His relatives surrounded him weeping and confirmed the story. He returned with them to the tree. The girl was gone—the bundle lay there—the young man fell *dead*." (*T*,3:126)

The diaries of Irving's western trip are of particular interest because he used them as the basis for his travel book *A Tour on the Prairies*. This use also suggests interesting parallels between this diary and Parkman's. A comparison between excerpts from two versions of the same incident, a raid on a honey tree, helps to reveal Irving's process of revision. The first version is from Irving's diaries, the second from *A Tour on the Prairies*:

Bees returning to their hive from abroad find the tree leveled and collect on the point of a withered branch of a neighboring tree, contemplating the ruin and buzzing about the downfall of their republic. (*T*,3:141)

It is difficult to describe the bewilderment and confusion of the bees of the bankrupt hive who had been absent at the time of the catastrophe and who arrived from time to time with full cargoes from abroad. At first they wheeled about in the air, in the place where the fallen tree had once reared its head, astonished at finding all a vacuum. At length, as if comprehending their disaster, they settled down in clusters on a dry branch of a neighboring tree, whence they seemed to contemplate the prostrate ruin, and to buzz forth doleful lamentations over the downfall of their republic.[23]

The basic imagery comparing the hive to a human state was established in the original; the revision benefits from the opportunity to polish the style and enhance details, but it also suffers from added ornamentation. In adapting his diaries Irving also altered facts and reduced the amount of dialogue. He kept other diaries after his return from the West. The last of these, written in 1842, describes a trip to Spain to serve an American minister. However, these diaries are rather brief.

John J. Audubon (1785–1851)

Though Audubon was born in Haiti and raised in France, I have classified the famous artist and naturalist as an American diarist. Audubon came to the United States when he was only eighteen, settled, and married here. However, even more significant for the purposes of this volume is his early and consistent identification of himself as an American.

There are a few extant entries from Audubon's diaries that were written as early as 1812, and these suggest that Audubon's record began earlier still; however, most of his first diaries were destroyed. The earliest reasonably complete section covers a trip to New Orleans in 1820–21, including material on his constant search for new birds to paint (most of Audubon's surviving journals were composed during periods of travel).[24] Other diaries of travels in the North American wilderness are those of a brief trip to Labrador in 1833 and a longer journey up the Missouri River in 1843.

These wilderness journals are extremely valuable for their information about Audubon's activities while seeking animal subjects for his art, but they are not among the better diaries of their type. Audubon's entries usually offer relatively straightforward renderings of the animals seen, caught, or killed and places visited. Only occasionally are there entries that give the reader insights into his character. In one Audubon looked at some trees by a river bank, "dying not through the influence of fire, the natural enemy of wood, but from the force of the mighty stream . . . which appeared as if in its wrath to undo all that the Creator in His bountifulness had granted to enjoy." This destruction he saw as "an awful exemplification of the real course of Nature's intention that all should and must live and die.[25]

In another entry he attempted to demythologize the midwestern prairie, insisting that to his eyes it was a "wild and . . . miserable country, the poetry of which lies in the imagination of those writers who have described the 'velvety prairies' and 'enchanted castles' (of mud) so common where we are now"(A, 2:14). Audubon showed that the destructive power of the wilderness was no harsher than the actions of the white trappers and settlers who brought smallpox and other diseases. Even the members of his own party despoiled the grave of an Indian chief and carried off the head (A, 1:72).

By the standards applied in this volume, the best of Audubon's diaries is not a wilderness diary but one written during his trip to Europe from 1826 to 1829. This European diary was written for his wife, Lucy; and, as in the following excerpt, he even included an occasional direct address to her: "I have looked upon thy likeness, sweet wife, very intently to-day and felt such an inclination to kiss it that my lips became burning hot and ——— oh sweet wife when will we meet again?" (F, 246) This focused audience and Audubon's sense of isolation from his family may have given this diary the unity and narrative interest that the other portions of his record lack.

When he went to Europe to arrange publication for his illustrations of wildlife, Audubon met with success beyond his expectation. He was repeatedly amazed by the favorable reception he met, especially the attention of the great men of England. He was awed when Lord Stanley, famous not only as a member of Parliament but also as a writer and naturalist, came to view his drawings, but he was put at ease when the "English lord" spread out the works on the floor and got down on his knees to view them (F, 83). In another entry he expressed his ambivalence about meeting with Sir Walter Scott: "Ah Walter Scott, when I am presented to thee my head will droop, my heart will swell, my limbs will tremble, my lips quiver, my tongue congeal. I shall be mute, and perhaps not even my eyes will dare turn towards thee, Great Man. Nevertheless I will feel elevated that I was permitted to touch thy hand" (F, 285–86). In some situations Audubon expressed anxiety in part because he felt he would be unable to respond forcefully to criticism: "Anyone would think me pusillanimous and all would wrong me. Have I not met and defeated the wild, voracious Panther, and the active Bear, attacked the Wolves during their slaughter, and defied the Wild Cat's anger. Ah yes, and again and again . . . but Lucy, to wound the heart of *Man* is beyond my courage" (*F,* 101).

Some parts of the diary show how Audubon arranged and painted his animal subjects, but a larger portion is devoted to accounts of tourist activity: castles, exhibits, scenery, paintings, hunts, meals, and the like. Yet Audubon was not the casual tourist. The attention that he had devoted to wild nature he turned to the appearance and behavior of men and human institutions. Manchester was "full of noise and tumult," and "the vast number of youth of both sexes with sallow complexions, ragged apparel, and downcast looks, made . . . [him] feel they were not as happy as the slaves of Louisiana" (*F,* 139).

In his paintings Audubon could take delight in the savage wildness of nature, "the 'Hawk' pouncing on seventeen partridges, the 'Whooping Crane' devouring alligators newly born . . . the Great-footed Hawks . . . with bloody rage at their beak's ends, and cruel delight in the glance of their daring eyes"; but he was horrified to find the same mindless cruelty in man (*F,* 249–50). He complained against the "infamous" treadmills of the Liverpool jail: "Conceive of a wild Squirrel within a round wheel, moving himself without progress. The labor is too severe, and the true motive of correction destroyed, as there are no mental resources attached to this laborious engine of shame" (*F,* 183–84). His conclusion was that the English would have done better if they had sought to improve the lot of the poor rather than to extend their empire (*A,* 1:240).

Being in London made Audubon feel as though he were in prison. It was not just that he preferred the beauty and freedom of the American wilderness, but that he felt that city especially antithetical to his own essence (*A,* 1:277). Indeed, the effect of the English capital was so strong that it even interfered with both his art and his journalizing (*A,* 1:258). England did have her beauties, but all too often Audubon found them marred by the hand of man in ways that made him long for the forests of America. In one entry he wrote: "Lucy, as you go to Park place the view up and over the Mersey is extensive and rather interesting. . . . This afternoon it afforded a calming moment of repose, to the eye, from the bustle of the street on the silent, faint, faraway mountains of Wales. Steam vessels moved swiftly in all directions on the Mersey, but they are not to be compared with ours of the [one and] only Ohio! No. They look like smoky floating dungeons, and I turn my sight from them" (*F,* 96–97).

Audubon was not totally opposed to industrialization. Viewing a mill, symbol of the industrial revolution, with its "great engine," he found the "stupendous structure" to be "so beautiful in all its parts that [he felt] no one could . . . stand and look at it without praising the ingenuity of man" (A, 1:246). However, for Audubon all of the virtues of the Old World could never equal those of the New (A, 1:240–41). While in Europe, his repeated wish was to be "in America's dark woods, admiring God's works in all their beautiful ways" (A, 1:235). His work accepted, Audubon made a brief visit to France, and then in April 1829, returned to America.

Other Exploration and Travel Diaries

There are far more fine diaries of exploration and travel written during this period than can be treated on these pages. Among those worthy of mention is that of Captain John R. Bell (1784–1825), the official journalist for the Stephen H. Long Expedition, which in 1820 explored the central portion of the Louisiana Territory. Bell's experience was similar to those of other exploration diarists in this chapter, and his long and well-written entries offer an opportunity for useful comparisons. A slightly different diary from those treated here is that of Thomas Nuttall, a pioneering botanist whose diaries won him a reputation and a Harvard professorship. His record was not merely a scientific document, but also a vivid portrait of the Indian and of early settlers. Nuttall, however, was less able than Audubon to qualify as an American diarist. He was born and raised in England; and, though he remained in America for many years, he returned to England to take up his inheritance.

Another British diarist, Frances Anne (Fanny) Kemble (1808–93), is so important in American diary literature that one might almost make an exception for her. One excuse for her inclusion would be the fact that, although she was born and died in England, Fanny Kemble was married for fifteen years (from 1834 until her divorce in 1849) to an American, Pierce Butler. However, to do so would violate the usual standards of this volume; the first of her two famous published diaries, *Journal of a Residence in America,* covers a period (1832–33) that was not only before her marriage but also before her first visit to the United States; the second diary, *Journal of a Residence on a Georgia Plantation 1838–1839,* covers a period only a few years later. Her point of view, even in the later period, cannot really be classed as American. Nevertheless, these diaries are too good, their influence on American society too significant, and their author too closely related to major American diarists to be totally ignored. Moreover, the publication of these diaries, the first in 1835 and the second in 1863, was important in affecting the conception of the diary form held by Americans of the period.

The first of Kemble's published diaries begins with her departure for America on August 1, 1832. In her first entry she wrote of leaving "all the world behind" and pledging to preserve some "dear English flowers" until she could once again "stand upon the soil on which they grew."[26] In one of her early entries she wrote of her willingness to trade a "surpassing" American sunset for "a wreath of English fog" (1:89). However, by the end of the work she seems almost to have forgotten home in her fascination with the new land; the final lines tell of her awe after rushing "to the brink of the abyss. I saw Niagra—Oh God! who can describe that sight?"(2:286–87).

Kemble was critical of many of the characteristics of Americans and their society, from their table manners to their pride in their democratic institutions. Typical was her insistence that there was "no such thing" as equality in America, for there as elsewhere people insisted on the privileges of status (1:72). Although she omitted names in her accounts, many of the people she discussed could be identified, and as a result the publication of the diary caused a good deal of reaction.[27]

However, none of her criticisms of her stay in the American Northeast was as severe as that which she wrote about her stay in Georgia. Only after her marriage did Kemble learn that, although her husband was from Philadelphia, the major part of his fortune was a plantation in the sea islands of Georgia worked by hundreds of slaves. Kemble, who on religious and moral grounds was a strong abolitionist, felt herself tainted as the recipient of benefits from the labor of slaves, and sought to visit the plantation so that she might learn about the situation and begin to remedy it.[28] At the very least she hoped to dispute her husband's claim that blacks were "*animals,* incapable of mental culture and moral improvement"(4).

Her diary of her experiences there was written in the form of letters addressed (but not sent) to a friend from Massachusetts, Elizabeth Dwight Sedgwick. Kemble gave a good account of the appearance and workings of the plantation, but her most vivid passages are about the slaves and their situation. In one entry she recorded the story of a young woman who was flogged when she was too ill to complete her work: "She described to me that they were fastened up by their wrists to a beam or branch of a tree, their feet barely touching the ground so as to allow them no purchase for resistance or evasion of the lash, their clothes turned over their heads, and their backs scored with a leather thong" (215). Kemble did not publish this dramatic diary until 1863, when she did so as part of an effort to weaken British support for the Confederacy.

Two other travel diaries, worthy of special notice both in their own right and for comparison with that of Washington Irving, are those of Theodore Dwight (1796–1866) and Thomas Cole (1801–48). Both men were involved in the arts, the former as a writer of histories and travel books and the latter as a painter; both wrote travel diaries, most of which were devoted to trips to Europe.

Dwight's *A Journal of a Tour in Italy in the Year 1821*[29] invites comparison with Irving's first diary of travel in Europe. For example, his impression of Naples was very much like that Irving had expressed sixteen years earlier. Dwight described a land of incredible beauty that is home to "the most wretched set of beings," a collection of rogues, beggars, servants, or serfs whose labors only enrich "the indolent and vicious landholder or the overflowing church or convent." Like Irving, Dwight was disturbed at seeing "walls of white marble . . . heaped up to the clouds and hung with the richest productions of art, [while] the mind of man is sunk in proportion and humbled to the very dust" (161, 165, 174).

Cole's diary begins a decade later than Dwight's, during a trip the painter had made to Europe to study art. In his poem "To Cole, the Painter Departing for Europe" the poet William Cullen Bryant had warned his friend against losing "that earlier, wilder image" of the American landscape when confronted with a Europe whose fairest scenes all bear "the trace of men." In one of his entries written in Europe, Cole himself expressed the fear that "intercourse with men" had had a "benumbing . . . effect on the soul" and deadened his "sense of the beautiful in nature.[30]

His diary shows that Cole need not have worried. Whether in Europe or back in America, like Irving before him, he looked with a Romantic eye upon human works and the wonders of nature, the "desolate sublimity" of "the ruin of an old Etruscan wall," the "desolate grandeur" of a "gulf fearfully deep" opening "with ridgy sides, into a vast and dreary plain ribbed with countless ravines" cut by "a scanty stream that struggles with many windings and turnings through the thirsty desert," until it "finally loses itself in the dark and more kindly distance" (96). Cole seems to have been almost incapable of long viewing such scenes without conceiving studies for new painting and beginning philosophical speculations. Indeed, in his diary Cole explained that he saw art and philosophy as linked: "Doubtless the true and the beautiful are one in art and nature"(251).

Chapter Four
Other Diaries of Situation

In most cases a diary has its origin in response to or in anticipation of some situation or incident that produces a dislocation in the diarist's life, and there may be as many different types of diaries as there are situations. Even when one tries to group these diaries into more general categories there are still a large number of distinct forms. Some, such as religious experiences or travel, tend to inspire large numbers of personal records, others comparatively few. The number of diaries in a given class may vary from society to society and period to period.

In some cases the reasons for this variation may be relatively clear. For example, large numbers of excellent war diaries were written during the American Revolution and the Civil War; a far smaller number were produced by Americans during the early nineteenth century. Among the reasons that the conflicts of this period, which included the War of 1812 and the Mexican War, produced so few diaries of literary value may be the size, length, and location of the conflict. Few civilians of this period were significantly and directly affected by these struggles, and the emotional involvement of American society was significantly lower than it was during either the Revolution or the Civil War.

Another reason a particular form has received little or no coverage in this volume may be that its best practitioners went on to create other diary forms. This is particularly true in the case of literary and artistic notebooks. We have already seen the case of Washington Irving, whose literary notebooks are embedded in a work that is more appropriately classified as a travel diary. As we shall see in a later chapter some writers, such as Emerson, used their skill to develop their literary notebooks into far more complex works that go beyond situation.

In the case of other diary forms the reasons are less obvious. Indeed, the only reason for their absence in this work may be chance variations in the literary talent of the diarists. When literary quality is the prime reason for selecting a small number of works from thousands, considerable variation in distribution is probable. Certainly, many diaries of romance and courtship and of politics were produced during the early nineteenth century, but few are as interesting or well written as those of James Gallatin or James K. Polk.

James Gallatin (1796–1876)

Only sixteen when he began his diary, James Gallatin had a writing skill beyond his years but a focus and set of values that betrayed his youth. James had gone to Europe in 1813 as secretary to his father, Albert Gallatin, who had been appointed as a commissioner to aid in a Russian effort to negotiate an end to the War of 1812. He was still in Europe when his father joined John Quincy Adams, Henry Clay, and others in negotiating the Treaty of Ghent.[1] William Matthews in his bibliography of American diaries classified Gallatin's record as a political diary, and the work was indeed begun to record a diplomatic mission; however, especially after a brief early section, Gallatin showed little concern about matters of diplomacy or politics. Exposed to some of the most important figures in the world, James focused his attention on grandeur rather than power, and on personality rather than event. After meeting Emperor Alexander of Russia, Gallatin spent some time recording in the diary the emperor's conversation on issues; but he seems to have been more concerned that to the emperor and others he "looked, very young".[2]

The reader will not mind Gallatin's youth because it made the diarist willing to recount details that an older man might have ignored. For example, going to Madame de Staël's,[3] Gallatin did not hesitate to record that she was "rather fat" and "oddly dressed" or to note that there were silver rests for knives and forks. He concluded his account of the evening by writing, "After about an hour we adjourned to the large gallery. All the ladies were seated stiffly around the room. Only one person talked at a time. It is called a *salon*. It was interesting at first, but after three hours of it I wished myself in Paris" (47). With this disarming candor he disposed of a major social institution. Gallatin was not even very interested in the sights or culture of a foreign land; his major concern was romantic intrigue.

Once in Paris, which he called the "paradise of young men," Gallatin predicted he would "soon be in mischief" and moved to make his prediction fact (90). In an entry typical of the light comedy of the diary Gallatin, telling about driving his "new 'curricle' for the first time," declared that he didn't know whether he or his horse "was the most proud." Gallatin's pride was not merely in his carriage but in its ability to attract attention. He wrote: "I saw many lovely ladies, and I flatter myself some of them saw me. I find they notice much more when I am driving than when I am on foot. Moral—always drive" (91).

After noticing the beauty of the French women, Gallatin again admitted his tendency to misbehave: "I shall get into all sorts of scrapes" (91). Eager for romantic adventures, he took up with a "charming little danseuse of the opera" (92), an encounter that was probably responsible for a three-month lapse in the diary. Then, breaking with her, he returned to formal dances with ladies of society. However, the restrictions of formal etiquette drove him back to less elegant entertainments. In one entry a young American art student introduced him to the *"grisette* world":[4]

My *grisette* ball was not a success—the fact is, it was not fit for any gentleman to go to; I am not particular but there are limits. The men were much worse than the women. How can they degrade themselves to such an extent! They left nothing to the imagination. I was determined to stay to the end, and even went to supper at a restaurant at the Halle. I will never forget the horrible orgie. There were Russian, Spanish, Italian, and Prussian students; they might have been wild beasts from their behavior. This has been a lesson to me; I am glad of the experience and will profit by it. (97)

Of course he was not reformed, as the reader finds a few entries later when Gallatin reveals a "most unpleasant adventure." Walking in the gardens of the Palais Royal, Gallatin smiled boldly at a pretty young woman. When his stares were answered with smiles, he assumed the lady a *grisette* and dropped a note to propose a rendezvous. Soon a reply was delivered, inviting him to call that evening. When he did so, he encountered the following scene:

An old woman met me at the door. Putting her finger to her lips and bidding me to follow her, she mounted to the second floor. Letting us in with a key, I found myself in the most beautiful apartment. She threw open the door, and to my amazement there was my *grisette* with a child of about two years on her lap and one a year or so older standing by her side. All were beautifully dressed, and sitting by a little table was a man. He rose, and with a bow said, "Monsieur, you are most welcome to our humble home. My wife has kept the children out of bed expressly for you to see them." Imagine my deep mortification. She is Mademoiselle R—— of the Théâtre Français. It was a lesson I will not forget and which I richly deserved. They both begged me to honour them with a visit at any time. (102–3)

Gallatin recorded several other such scrapes, which have so much of the character of romantic farce that only the age of the writer and the naive simplicity of his narration prompt the reader to believe that they are factual. In one such incident he had arranged a romantic liaison with "a certain lady of the *grand monde,*" and had taken her to "the most unlikely place in the world to meet anybody," when "Horror of horrors!" who should he spy but his mother (173). Another assignation was interrupted by the unexpected arrival of the woman's lover:

I had rather an unfortunate adventure some few nights since, but it I hope will never get to father's ears. After going to the opera, a charming little *danseuse,* whose acquaintance I had only just made, asked me if I would sup with her at her apartment. Much to my surprise I found the greatest luxury— some personage evidently in the background. A round table with *couverts* for two. We had just commenced to sup when I heard a noise in the antechamber. My charmer exclaimed, *"Mon Dieu, je suis perdue, cachez-vous."* I rushed behind a curtain. The door opened, and to my dismay I recognized the voice of the Duc de Berri. He said, "So mademoiselle has an *amant."* Clare tremblingly answered, *"Non, Monseigneur,* it was only mamma who I was giving a little supper to as you did not arrive." He asked, "What has become of her?" "She has gone, Monseigneur, as she was not properly dressed to receive your Highness." By bad luck I had left my hat on a chair. The Duke picked it up and said with a laugh, "So, madame, *votre mère* wears a man's hat, which she has forgotten." I felt it was time for me to discover myself, no matter what the consequences might be. I stepped out from behind the curtain, saying, "Monseigneur, it is my hat; I am mademoiselle's mother." He broke into fits of laughter, poor Clare into tears. He laughed so heartily that I could not help joining him; he then became serious and in the kindest manner said, "Young man, you have acted in a most honourable manner not to play eavesdropper. *Tout est pardonné.* Let us sup together." Clare rang and ordered another *couvert* to be laid, and we had a most cheerful supper. When he rose to leave he begged me to accompany him, which, of course, I did. Going down the stairs he took me by the arm and said most kindly, "I am really the one to blame; here we have met as Mr. Smith and Mr. Jones," adding, "in fact, you have unknowingly done me a great favour, as I was most anxious to get rid of Mlle. Clare; you have given me the opportunity. I am your debtor, but do not forget I am Mr. Smith." (107–8)

The literary cliché of the hidden lover and the forgotten article of clothing gains new life in the real world of the diary, but the anecdote depends for its success on Gallatin's tone, which keeps the comic and serious possibilities in balance. On a wider scale this balance is essential to the diary as a whole. Gallatin makes the reader aware that the context of such comic adventures is a world of deadly earnest in which executions, duels, assassination plots, and political conspiracies are relatively common. He helps us to understand that there is a relation between such political instability and the inconsistency of moral and social standards. His diary is a logical companion to the diary written by Governeur Morris during his time as American ambassador to France. Its entries deal with situations like those Morris had described in his diary a quarter of a century earlier.[5]

On a personal level, a serious theme of the diary is the conflict between James's adventures and his parents' values and behavior. In the same entry with his account of the *grisette* ball Gallatin wrote of his father: "He does not mind how much I go out in the *grand monde* but he dislikes anything like low life. He never had a youth himself; he was penned up in Geneva" (97). The formality of the elder Gallatin's life is indicated in his son's diary by a reference to his refusal of an extremely lucrative partnership with John Jacob Astor because he could never place himself on the same level with a "butcher's son" who ate "peas with a knife" (80). James's mother's strong religious principles were indicated by her refusal to attend court functions on the sabbath. Her attempts to treat James as a child provided a background for his acts of rebellion.

While the formality and standards of his parents conflicted with James's behavior, they allow the reader to anticipate and understand his eventual turning away from "indiscretions" and assuming the responsibilities of a "respectable life." True to these expectations, Gallatin in 1823 met the daughter of an expatriate French marquis then living in Baltimore and declared, "I have never seen anything more lovely" (245). Two days later he announced in the diary, "I am without a doubt in love with her" (246). In a little more than a month the couple was engaged. Gallatin continued to write in his diary until 1827; however, during these years he made comparatively few entries. This decline and eventual end of diary production offer further evidence that its primary function was to deal with a period of youthful courtship. The diary ended as James Gallatin had begun to assume his position in society and the responsibilities that went with it.

James K. Polk (1795–1849)

Polk's diary is a true political diary, almost totally devoted to chronicling his political activity and running concurrently with his presidency. On August 26, 1845, twenty-five weeks after his inauguration as president, James K. Polk met with Secretary of State James Buchanan to discuss the settlement of the Oregon boundary. The account that Polk wrote in order to preserve a distinct memory of that meeting "suggested . . . the idea if not the necessity of keeping a journal or diary of events and transactions . . . [of his] presidency." Although he sometimes found himself "so much engaged with . . . public duties as to be able to make only a very condensed and imperfect statement of events . . . and to be forced to omit others altogether," the daily record he began the next day is remarkably full and regular.[6] Indeed, on some occasions when he found nothing of significance to record, Polk entered that fact in his diary.

Conceiving the diary as an official record, Polk first referred to himself in the third person. There were only a few lapses in this practice during the first two months, but after that point Polk shifted to the first-person style of most diaries. This shift involved more than a stylistic change. The entries began to involve some personal material not associated with the official business, and even the treatment of official activities included more subjective reflections. It may be significant that Polk intended to keep the diary after leaving office, but no final determination can be made because Polk died about three months after the end of his term. Nevertheless, this continuation is further evidence that the diary had become far more than an official record.

One constant source of irritation Polk faced was the stream of visitors who came seeking donations, loans, and handouts. He wrote in the diary:

I am applied to almost daily & sometimes half a dozen times a day for money, by persons who do not ask it for charitable purposes, but by well dressed persons, men and women. They call on me to contribute to build Academies, to aid colleges, and for churches in every part of the Union. . . . The idea seems to prevail with many persons that the President is from his position compelled to contribute to every loafer who applies, provided he represents that the sum he wants is to build a church, an academy, or a college. (2:28)

Even worse than those who came seeking money were those who sought appointments to federal positions for themselves or their friends. In one entry Polk complained:

My office was crowded up to the hour of 12 O'Clock with visitors, and I was greatly annoyed by the importunities of office-seekers. It is most disgusting to be compelled to spend hour after hour almost every day in hearing the applications for office made by loafers who congregate at Washington, and by members of Congress in their behalf, and yet I am compelled to submit to it or offend or insult the applicants and their friends. The people of the U.S. have no idea of the extent to which the President's time, which ought to be devoted to more important matters, is occupied by the voracious and often unprincipled persons who seek office. If a kind Providence permits me length of days and health, I will, after I retire from the Presidential office, write the secret and hitherto unknown history of the workings of the Government in this respect. I[t] requires great patience & self command to repress the loathing I feel towards a hungry crowd of unworthy office-hunters who often crowd my office. (3:418–19)

Polk did not live long enough to compile such a formal history, but his diary constitutes an excellent informal one. These office seekers were incredibly persistent. They would sneak into the president's office even when he had "directed that no one be admitted." In one instance, within an hour after the rumor of the death of one officeholder, the first applicant for the position had already arrived (4:274). Polk, as a Jacksonian Democrat, continued to support the principle behind this "spoils system" with its political appointments while he complained about its practical effects.

So great was the stream of applicants that when a day passed without a "single office seeker," Polk considered that fact a "remarkable" event worth recording in his diary (2:113). Many of his closest political associates became office seekers. In one series of entries Senator Thomas Hart Benton came in suggesting conceitedly that "commissioners composed of the first men in the country . . . should accompany the army in the Mexican War." Then four days later Benton suggested the creation of a "general in chief" to supersede all present officers and nominated himself for the post (2:222, 227).[7]

Polk seems to have had little "literary" interest in characterization, but his strong though frequently uninformed or politically influenced attitudes toward others produced many vivid comments. In one series of entries the fate of a tariff bill, one of the main pieces of legislation of Polk's administration, hung on the vote of one senator, Jarnigan of Tennessee. Polk feared that Jarnigan, despite his previous declaration of support, might oppose the measure. When the senator explained, "in a serious & emphatic tone that his vote was no secret, that he was instructed to vote for just such a Bill as this was, and that he should do so," Polk claimed to have no more doubts. However, Polk concluded his discussion of Jarnigan's vote by writing, "If he votes as he declared he would to-day, the Bill will still pass" (2:47–48). The word *if* indicates that the diarist was only partially convinced. In the entries of the next few days Polk showed that the vacillating Jarnigan did shift his stand; in successive votes he turned against the bill, abstained and, finally, supported it.

Such incidents as recorded in the diary are significant not only because they suggest that Polk thought his positions were superior, but also because Polk repeatedly showed himself unable to accept opposing views as rational or honest. In the diary Polk denounced the Wilmot Proviso, which banned slavery from any territory to be gained in a treaty ending the Mexican War, as "mischievous and foolish" because he could not conceive of any connection between "making peace with Mexico" and slavery (2:75).

The diary gives an excellent behind-the-scenes view of politics, allowing the reader to see not only the secret intrigues, but also the factors of personality that influence administrative decisions. An excellent example of such a complex political situation appears in entries about the appointment of a Supreme Court justice. The incident is particularly interesting because it involved one of Polk's most important cabinet officers, Secretary of State James Buchanan. The vacancy had existed under the previous administration and, at that time, had been offered to Buchanan, who then rejected it.[8]

Without direct comment Polk allows readers of the diary to see the real positions behind his diplomatically worded conversation with Buchanan. In these entries Buchanan did not at first ask for the post; rather, he introduced the issue by disclaiming responsibility for a rumor that he wanted the post and then suggested that the appointment might be to the advantage of Polk's program. Polk, however, turned the "suggestion" aside by speaking about Buchanan's importance in his present role (1:47). Less than two months later Buchanan reintroduced the subject by announcing his decision not to ask for the judgeship while at the same time explaining that "he would rather be chief justice of that court than . . . President." Then, perhaps recognizing the implications of such a statement, he added that "he did not desire to be President and never had." Polk, however, had already recognized Buchanan's new goal and responded by explaining "I would take no part in selecting the candidate of my party to succeed me, but would leave that to my political friends; I stated further my belief that no man would ever be elected President who was prominently before the Public for that office two or three years or a longer time before the nomination" (1:97–98).

The situation did not end with this exchange. Buchanan next took up the cause of another candidate for the vacancy. When Polk rejected that choice, Buchanan, or so Polk's informant suggested, worked to defeat Polk's nominee and then seemed again to be seeking the part for himself:

I learned . . . that it was the common talk at Mr. Buchanan's Ball last night that he (Mr. B.) was to go on the Bench of the Supreme Court, in place of Mr. Woodward rejected. I learned, too, that there is another rumour in the streets that Mr. Buchanan will soon leave the Cabinet. These rumours are strange to me. I have reason to believe that Mr. Buchanan is dissatisfied, but if so he has no reason for it unless it be that I make my own appointments to office, according to my best judgment, and will not suffer him to dispense the public patronage. . . . I have done Mr. B. full justice, and have given to his peculiar friends even more than their proportion of the offices, because he was a member of my Cabinet & I was desirous to satisfy him by giving him evidence that I had friendly feelings towards him. With this I fear he is not satisfied. His greatest weakness is his great sensitiveness about appointments to office. He has repeatedly seemed to be troubled, & taken it greatly to heart when I have differed with him on appointments & made my own selections. Being responsible for my appointments, I cannot surrender the appointing power to any one else, and if, because I will not do so, Mr. B. chooses to retire from my Cabinet I shall not regret it. (1:189–90)

When, finally, Polk offered to appoint Buchanan at the end of the current session of Congress, the secretary first demanded an immediate appointment and a month later withdrew his candidacy.[9]

It is through such groups of entries that Polk provides his readers with insights into the various "characters" in the diary. Of course, Polk seems to have had "little literary" intention, but there are many motives for effective characterizations in diary literature. Polk used his diary in a number of ways that benefited by such characterization.

Polk's diary served to provide him with an outlet for the emotional strain of the presidency. He felt that his position did not allow him to politely "descend" into certain controversies, but he was able to satisfy his desire to make his position known by using his diary to record "a brief statement of facts so they may not be unknown if . . . the proper occasion arises" (4:40–41).

Perhaps the key to Polk's diary is his early decision to be a one-term president. This point is repeated throughout the diary. On his fifty-second birthday he wrote, "I have now passed through two-thirds of my Presidential term, & most heartily wish that the remaining third was over, for I am sincerely desirous to have the enjoyment of private life" (3:210). In rejecting a second term, Polk not only sought to free himself from the pressure to take actions according to their potential effect on a future campaign, but also to focus any hope for a successful record on that one term. The diary, both in form and content, shows its author's consistent effort toward that end.

Polk's single term was an especially busy one, including a major war, significant territorial acquisitions, and tariff changes, as well as a continuation and extension of other controversies such as that concerning slavery. Polk asserted in the diary his intention to assume full responsibility for these actions. The diary suggests that Polk was unwilling to delegate powers even to his senior officials, trusting, sometimes with justification, that his own judgment was superior to theirs. One such incident involved his disagreement with Buchanan about a letter to be sent to the emperor of Brazil: "I then jocosely said to him [Buchanan], I will stand you a basket of champaign that this letter is not in the usual form as you insist, and that the precedents in the State Department will not sustain it. He promptly said, Done, I take you up, and rising in a fine humour, said, now I will go over to the Department & bring the precedents." When Buchanan was unable to find a precedent and insisted on paying the wager, Polk added:

I smiled and told him I would not accept it, and that I had been jesting when I proposed [it], and had done so only to express in an earnest manner my conviction that I was right. But, he said, if I had won it I would have made you pay it, & I will pay it to you. I repeated that I would not accept it. I record this incident for the purpose of showing how necessary it is for me to give my vigilant attention even to the forms & details of my [subordinates'] duties. (3:98–99)

Such attention to forms and details and to the multitude of visitors and applicants seriously taxed Polk's strength. He died the very same year that he left office. Had he lived, his diary might well have developed into a true life diary.

Chapter Five
Life Diaries

One problem in classifying the diaries that were written in nineteenth-century America lies in distinguishing between diaries of situation and life diaries. The most common diary is, like the ones we have been considering, a diary of situation, a work created to record a special activity or to perform a limited role. The life diary is a more complex form. While some diaries have been begun as life diaries, more often a life diary had its origin as a diary of situation; then at some point its entries began to go beyond the boundaries of a single function or even any specified group of functions, and the diary started to determine its own subject matter. In the life diary the act of diary keeping is the main reason for its production.

Diaries of situation may and usually do contain material unrelated to their primary motive, and life diaries may for periods focus on only a limited subject. Just as there are types of situation diaries that are similar to or overlap others, so life diaries may, for periods, seem like diaries of situation. While over an extended number of entries the basic form of a diary is usually sufficiently clear and consistent for a reader to assign it to one of the two types, if one examines only sections the controlling motive may not be clear. In some life diaries, such as that of Philip Hone, no single motive dominates for any extensive period, but in others the entries may, like their authors' lives, tend to be concentrated on some particular concern. For example, in the colonial period Cotton Mather wrote a life diary that was more involved with spiritual concerns than with any others. In the nineteenth century John Quincy Adams wrote a diary that, like its author, was most often involved with politics and was frequently dominated by any of a number of other concerns such as travel. And, as we shall see in the next chapter, the diaries of Emerson and Alcott involve still more complex motives. However, a careful reading of long sections of any of these works should still suggest that the process of diary keeping became the heart of diary production.

Philip Hone (1780–1851)

Though his family had little money, by the time he was forty Philip Hone had amassed such a fortune that he was able to retire from business. The balance of his life was spent as a leading figure in New York society and as an occasional politician (he even served as mayor for one year, 1825–26).[1] His lavish parties attracted many of the most fashionable New Yorkers as well as some of the famous visitors to that city, allowing Hone to record encounters with presidents and senators as casually as most men might write about a routine business meeting. A list of the important Americans who figure prominently in Hone's diary is too long to include here, but among the most famous were John Jacob Astor, John Quincy Adams, James Fenimore Cooper, Washington Irving, and Martin Van Buren.[2]

During his term as mayor Hone began a commonplace book, including such items as lists of aldermen and copies of speeches; however, by the end of 1828 the work had matured into a well-developed diary that would last almost until his death twenty-three years later and run to over two million words. Hone found diary keeping a pleasure rather than a "task" because it had become so much of a habit that it seemed a part of his existence, and he recognized that it might yield benefits not only for himself if he ever reread earlier entries, but also for others, who might learn from it "how he thought and 'what he did' about these times" (1:37). Hone certainly met these objectives.

Hone paid considerable attention to the various advantages of diary keeping. For example, in one passage in which he commented on John Quincy Adams's practice Hone explained that although Adams had "an unfailing memory, rendered stronger by cultivation," the fact that "he was never mistaken" and that "none disputed his authority" was to a considerable extent the result of his habit of diary keeping, through which "every circumstance of his long life was 'penned down' at the moment of its occurrence" (*T*, 2:342).

Like John Winthrop's diary, Hone's is a relatively impersonal chronicle of his time; but, unlike Winthrop, Hone made no attempt to disguise his own interest and involvement in the events he recorded. He was particularly astute about recognizing the events and trends that would prove important in determining the major direction of American culture. He was especially impressed by the technology of the "age of invention" in which he lived. In 1830 he noted his amazement at learning that "one of the locomotive engines on the Liverpool and Manchester railroad traversed the distance between the two places, thirty-two miles, in thirty-three minutes—*about fifty-eight miles an hour!*" (1:29). In 1838 he praised the size and speed of the *Great Western,* "The largest vessel propelled by steam which has yet made her appearance in the waters of Europe," after it had crossed the Atlantic in fifteen days (1:316).

Yet Hone was equally aware of the dangers of such power. Only a week after the arrival of the *Great Western* he lamented "the loss of 190 people on the *Moselle*" near Cincinnati, "the most shocking disaster on board a steamboat which has yet been recorded" (1:320). This disaster was soon followed by others which made Hone wonder if "Fulton's great invention will not prove a curse rather than a blessing to mankind" (*T,* 1:317). In a much later entry he wrote: "*Steam.* This powerful agent which regulates the affairs of the world, this new element, which like the other four is all-potent for good and for evil . . . has become a substitute for war in the philosophical plan for keeping down the super abundance of the human race. . . . Scarcely a day passes that we do not hear of some steamboat being blown up . . . or of a locomotive running off the railroad" (2:598).

Hone's diary includes early glimpses at other inventions such as the "*Magnetic Telegraph.* [A] Strange and wonderful discovery, which has made the 'swift winged lightning' man's messenger, annihilated all space and tied the two ends of the continent in a knot" (2:773), and the daguerreotype, which could make so perfect a photograph that "every object, however minute, is a perfect transcript of the thing itself; the hair of the human head, the gravel on the roadside, the texture of a silk curtain or the shadow of the smaller leaf reflected upon the wall are all imprinted as carefully as nature or art has created them." Such achievements led Hone to exclaim, "How greatly ashamed of their ignorance the by-gone generations of mankind ought to be!" His diary allows the reader to appreciate how people must have felt at learning about the creation of such marvels (1:435).

While Hone's comments on such inventions are important as indications of the rapid changes in science and technology that took place during his life, his accounts of changes in the social and political organization of America are at least as significant, and Hone was better suited by his experience and interests to chronicle these changes than those that resulted from technological improvements. Among the most striking features of the period that Hone described were the dramatic effects of rapid economic growth. The following excerpt is just one of many that convey the great wealth and power of the young American nation: "There was never a more beautiful Christmas than this day . . . Broadway from the Battery to Union Place has been an animated scene of new bonnets with happy faces under them, and little gentlemen and ladies bending under the weight of toys . . . and shops disregarding the injunction 'lead me not into temptation' spreading their tempting treasures . . . [as an] attraction to the coin in the pockets of the pas-sers-by" (2:641). Even Hone seems to have been astonished by the rate of growth in America: "Pulling down and rebuilding is the fashion of the day. It seems as if all the world has entered into a combination to exhaust the quarries of granite" (2:174). Hone shows that such feverish development had its negative side. Real estate speculation was so ex-treme that the land under buildings destroyed by fire might sometimes be sold for more than the property had been worth before the disaster.

Such inflation was not limited to the price of real estate. Hone com-plained about butter priced at "two shillings fourpence per pound" (1:185); and, in one entry, he gave a whole list of inflated prices not only to show their rise, but also in prophetic anticipation of a contin-uing inflation that might make what he saw as exorbitant seem cheap:

I record for future observation the cost of my marketing this morning. I could not do with less. It may cease to be a wonder hereafter for aught I know, but it is ruinous now:

A bass weighing fourteen pounds	$2.50
Two small turkey	$3.50
Three pairs chickens 4 pounds each	$3.37
One pair partridges (forbidden)	$1.00
Ordinary hind-quarter veal, 21 pounds	$3.95

(1:243)

Inflation was just one factor leading to the great panics of the 1830s and 1840s. Hone's record is full of descriptions of these great disrup-tions and complaints against the political policies that led to them. In the panic of 1833 he complained against "General Jackson's ill-advised measure of removing the public money from the Bank of the United States," an action which had "occasioned great distress." Interest rates were rising, and stocks falling, so that there were "bankruptcies and ruin in many quarters where a few short weeks since the sun of pros-perity shone with unusual brightness" (1:106–7). Hone compared the failure of one brokerage on Wall Street to the Battle of New Orleans: "His [Jackson's] killed and wounded were to be seen in every direction, and men enquiring with anxious solicitude, 'Who is to fall next?'" (1:112).

In the Great Panic of 1837 Hone early gave up recording the names of failed businesses because he saw that they were "only the forerunners of greater disasters" (1:250). He himself suffered greatly. Though his property was "nominally worth as much as it ever was," he could not convert it into cash to pay his debts except at ruinous prices and found himself forced to "put my pride in my empty pocket" and "like other poor devils, to bow to men who have money in their hands" (1:234).

Even without these personal problems Hone, as a strong supporter of the Whig Party, would hardly have remained neutral to the effects of Jackson's policies. Hone ran for or considered seeking a number of political offices, and he gave a good description of the chaotic politics of the period. In one entry written after an election won by the Democrats he complained: "I was kept awake during the greater part of the night by the unmanly insults of the ruffian crew from Tammany Hall who came over to my door every half hour and saluted me with groans and hisses . . . and for what? Because I have exercised the right . . . [to argue against] measures which I conceive to be dangerous to the liberties of the people" (1:141).

Such mob actions were all too common in the period. Hone wrote of riots in theaters and mass destruction in the streets. He was acutely aware of the destructive potential of the controversies related to slavery and by 1850 was already predicting that "the dreadful question of slavery" was leading to civil war. He felt that the actions by both "the fanatics of the North and the disunionists of the South had created "an enmity so fierce that reason can not allay it; unconquerable sectional jealousy" so strong that no compromise could be accepted, and "a dissolution of the Union, which until now was treason to think of, much more to utter, is the subject of daily harangues" (2:884).

Yet Hone had strong patriotic feelings. In describing a trip to Lexington and Concord to see a celebration of the first battles of the Revolution, Hone, who had gone as a guest of the governor, remarked that the day "must be marked with a white stone," an expression he reserved for "the pleasantest experiences" of his life because every event was "so decidely American" with "no foreign influence." Among the things he noted were a monument over "the bones of the first martyrs" to the "glorious cause of American independence," and "an excellent oration spoken by the Rev. Ralph Waldo Emerson, a young clergyman of distinguished talents and eloquence . . . full of interesting details relative to the first settlement of Concord," services which "partook of the spirit of the olden times, and a dinner with "about four hundred as honest-looking Yankees as ever sat down to eat cold roast pig" (1:175–77).

That Hone was very proud of the particular strengths of the young nation is also evident in the following anecdote: "I was forcibly stricken this morning of a characteristic circumstance of which an American can be proud. Passing through the crowd . . . was to be seen an elderly gentleman dressed in black, but not remarkably well dressed, with a mild, benignant countenance, a military air, but stooping a little, bowing to one, shaking hands with another, and cracking a joke with a third. And this man was William H. Harrison, the President-elect" (2:529).

While, as this excerpt indicates, ordinary men might occasionally meet a president, few men had the social and political connections that gave Hone the opportunity to make close observations of the most important men of his age. Many of the incidents that he recorded are all the more interesting because of the famous individuals involved. In one early entry Hone described a street brawl involving the poet William Cullen Bryant: "While shaving this morning at eight o'clock I witnessed . . . an encounter in the street nearly opposite between William C. Bryant, one of the editors of the *Evening Post,* and William L. Stone, editor of the *Commercial Advertiser.* The former commenced the attack by striking Stone over the head with a cowskin; after a few blows the parties closed and the whip was wrested from Bryant and carried off by Stone" (1:40).

This fight occurred in the street where anyone might have seen it; but, in the case of many other incidents, Hone was able to record them only because of his particular friendships and place in society. Some of his contacts with the famous were formal, like his encounters with Dickens when that novelist was honored in New York. However, Hone could invite Daniel Webster over to dine and refer to Henry Clay as "my distinguished friend" (1:102, 249). Washington Irving would attract such crowds when he appeared in public that "the men pressed on to shake his hand, and the women to touch the hem of his garment"; yet Hone could speak of him as a close acquaintance: "I have found him a most delightful companion. He is cheerful, gay, talkative, and appears no longer subject to those moody fits which formerly obscured his fine intellect at times, as the dark clouds flit across the face of the brightest summer's day. . . . I consider it fortunate that I invited him to be my roommate [on this trip], and I presume he does also" (1:89–90).

Hone earned these friendships, not only because of his position or hospitality, but also because of his judgment. He was, for example, among the first to recognize the genius of Thomas Cole. Hone told how Cole first came to New York, "full of undying ardor in the pursuit of knowledge, a lover of nature with a conscious ability for the portraiture of her features." "Unacquainted with the artistical quality of humbug," Cole had not been able to sell his paintings, but Hone quickly bought two, priding himself that those "*dilettanti,* who could not formerly discover $10 worth of merit in these early productions of the artist, would now be glad to buy [them] at a cost of $600 or $800" (2:837).

His closeness to these figures allowed him to make important comments about many famous men, but it is Hone's style and wit that make the portraits in his diary so interesting. For example, eulogizing John Quincy Adams, Hone wrote that "he 'talked like a book' on all subjects. Equal to the highest, the planetary system was not above his grasp. Familiar with the lowest, he could explain the mysteries of a mouse trap" (2:841).

Although Hone's social and political life made him a very "public" man, he was reticent about exposing his private life or uncensored personal feelings. After reading a portion of Fanny Kemble's *Journal of a Residence in America* that appeared in a newspaper, Hone wrote in his own diary that he could not "believe she ever intended it should see the light." It was not just that it contained, "all the light gossip, the childish prejudice, the hasty conclusions from first impressions, in which the diary of an imaginative youthful traveler in a country in which all things are new and untried may be supposed to abound," but that she must find it "'a sorry sight' to see herself thus served up to the public gaze" (*T,* 1:126). Hone certainly would have looked with displeasure on the prospect of having his diary published, even though it contains far less revealing personal information than do most such records.

Hone did include some very revealing passages, however. Some involved financial worries such as those which came as he tried to face the deterioration of his fortune that resulted from the wave of panics during the late 1830s and the early 1840s. On his sixtieth birthday he wrote: "I am doomed to vexations and troubles arising from pecuniary embarrassments for the remainder of my life" (1:505), and less than ten weeks later, "I cannot find a spot on the page of history marked in the margin 1840 on which to place a 'white stone.' My debts have increased, and my property is reduced in value, while those who owe me cannot or will not pay, and there is but little hope that they ever will" (*T*, 2:55).

Perhaps the most revealing passages are those few in which he felt the need to use his diary to express his feelings for his family beyond those statements in which he expressed his general thankfulness for their love and support. One such set of entries deals with the death of his daughter, Mary Hone Schermerhorn:

Friday was a melancholy day. The body was deposited in its coffin and placed in the back parlor. After the family had gone to bed, I obtained the key of the room and taking a lamp went into the chamber of death, seated myself at the side of the cold remains of my darling child, and for half an hour held in imagination delightful converse with the spirit which had of late animated it. . . . It is strange that I could derive consolation from looking upon the wreck of that which my heart held so dear, and yet it was a half hour of delightful enjoyment. (1:510–11)

On April 30, 1851, as Hone was finishing the last pages of a manuscript journal book, he wondered if he would have the strength to continue his diary: "Feeble beyond description, utterly destitute of appetite, with no strength in my limbs and no flesh on my bones, shall this journal be resumed?" It was his last dated entry. He added only an explanation of his choice for an epitaph and questioned, "Has the time come?" He died five days later (2:916–17).

John Quincy Adams (1767–1848)

In both style and content John Quincy Adams's diary is an exceptional work of literature. The work is rich in history thanks to Adams's presence at or involvement in many of the most significant events of his era such as Napoleon's return from Elba and the development of the Monroe Doctrine. Moreover, Adams met and dealt with many of the most important figures in the first half of the nineteenth century, including almost every American politician of note and many foreign leaders. The entries are full and regular and are written in a style so rich and varied that even trivial details become entertaining.

Nevertheless, because it is nearly three million words long, most of those who encounter it will probably be most struck by its quantity rather than its quality.[3] Few readers are prepared to undertake such a huge work, but the briefer abridgments available fragment the diary. There is, however, another alternative. Although a true life diary develops an identity that transcends any series of events or activities such as wars and travel, the diarist is often so influenced by those events that he/she develops subordinate patterns. Just as Faulkner's Yoknapatawpha novels stand as individual works yet fit together in a series, so sections of Adams's diary can be considered separately. The reader of such a section can rely on an abridgment to provide a sense of context. This procedure is useful for many of the large life diaries.

In the case of Adams's diary there are seven obvious major sections: an early diary of his trip to Europe with his father, a record kept during his law studies, next two diplomatic/travel sections separated by a portion covering Adams's term in the Senate, then a section dealing with Adams's terms as secretary of state and president, and finally one that treats his last years in Congress. Each section has its own themes and crises, but each follows a consistent major theme, the tension between a desire for external acceptance and an uncompromising moral sense. One cannot with confidence assert that there is a simple key to a diary of such physical and temporal length; yet even an imperfect generalization can prove useful.

Both Adams's life and his diary were shaped by his methodical persistence in the pursuit of principle; he had a vision of himself and his diary as models of virtue heroic in the face of adversity. Like his father, John Adams, John Quincy Adams felt that the choice of a path of virtue was crucial; but, compared to his father, John Quincy was less secure in his judgment and less confident of his power. His diary stresses the seriousness of the problems he and his country faced, but in seeking to overcome them Adams almost always favored certainty over speed and principle over pragmatism. Sharing his father's strength of conviction, but lacking his impulsiveness, John Quincy relied on comprehensive knowledge and patient care.

Whether engaged in diplomatic negotiations and political maneuvering or merely social conversation, Adams strove to control every detail and to be aware of the implications of every word. In one entry he noted how his caution helped him to avoid a diplomatic blunder. In a casual conversation the Russian czar had praised snow because "it made roads in the winter better than any that could be made by human art," helping to hold together an empire "so extensive that size was one of its great evils." Adams almost joked that, "great as this evil was, his Majesty had recently increased it" by annexing Finland. Fortunately, before speaking, Adams realized "the remark might be taken ill in part, or at least thought too familiar . . . [and he] suppressed it" (2:54–55).

Adams's concern for detail may help to account for the completeness of his diary entries. He bolstered his useful knowledge by carefully observing and recording in detail encounters and experiences. That he looked to his diary as a means to reflect on valuable experience seems supported by his practice of first writing regular daily entries and then summarizing sections on the first day of a month or year.

Many diarists have commented on the nature and techniques of their art, but few have done so as frequently as did Adams, who felt that diary keeping was a very special process worthy of great attention. He noted when the diary ran in arrears or lapsed and offered instructions on the ways to keep such a record. Perhaps Adams was so concerned with the nature of the diary form because it provided a bridge between the practical political career that took most of his time and the pursuit of the pure arts and sciences that was his constant interest.

The earliest printed volume of the diary begins as Adams, then twelve years old, accompanies his father on a series of diplomatic missions in Europe during and shortly after the American Revolution. In general, Adams's accounts are brief and impersonal in marked contrast to those of Gallatin, who went to Europe with his father on a similar mission. A second volume, published under the title *Life in a New England Town 1787–1788,* offers much of interest, but it is less accomplished than later sections. The attitudes Adams expressed are remarkably similar to those in his father's diary of a comparable period. Here we find the concern over future reputation and condemnations over inadequate progress toward the skills necessary for that attainment. A typical entry is the following:

The question, what am I to do in this world? recurs to me very frequently; and never without causing great anxiety, and a depression of spirits. My prospects appear darker to me every day, and I am obliged sometimes to drive the subject from my mind and to assume some more agreeable train of thought. I do not wish to look into futurity; and were the leaves of fate to be opened before me, I should shrink from the perusal. Fortune, I do not covet. Honours, I begin to think are not worth seeking, and as for 'the bubble reputation,' though deck'd with all the splendors of the rainbow, yet those very splendors are deceitful, and it seldom fails to burst from the weight of the drop which it contains. (*L,* 71)

Certainly effort and intelligence were not lacking; yet, like his father, he had such high expectations that he viewed a delay in an achievement as a reason for self-condemnation. In one entry he wrote: "I go but little into company, and yet I am not industrious. I am recluse, without being studious; and I find myself equally deprived of the pleasures of society, and of the sweet communion with the mighty dead. I am no stranger to the midnight lamp; yet I observe not that I make a rapid progress in any laudable pursuit" (*L,* 84).

The diary shows that the young John Quincy Adams was not totally puritanical; it shows him nursing an occasional hangover after excessive drinking or spending an evening socializing with the opposite sex. It prepares the reader to see Adams as human even considering the extraordinary achievements of his later life.

The first extensive section of the diary published in the *Memoirs* brings the young John Quincy Adams from a private law practice into the Europe of the French Revolution as ambassador to Holland. By this point Adams was already so skilled as a diarist that momentous events were not needed to create an interesting diary. When on a single page he condoned tipping and expressed astonishment at the execution of Robespierre, the contrast proves at least as instructive as the events described. The near-theft of a trunk which happened to contain diplomatic dispatches occasioned an entry so long (almost two thousand words) and so intricately self-revealing that even an extensive excerpt cannot do justice to the whole (2:41–45). The entries written during Adams's missions to Holland, Britain, and Prussia contain engaging depictions of the social life and diplomats in Europe, but their true vitality is apparent even in accounts of minor events. Nevertheless, the diary of this period had not yet developed the sense of continuity of theme which would make it distinguished.

In 1801 Adams was recalled to the Senate of the United States. The diary of his years as a senator is readable and gives a good portrait of the workings of the Congress, complete with accounts of impeachment trials and constitutional amendments. However, through most of this period it was the events in Congress that provided the direction of the diary; the control and personality of the author were only weakly established.

Then on June 30, 1807, Adams "first heard of an occurrence of very gloomy complexion—a new outrage from a British armed ship and the disgrace of one of our own frigates" (1:468). This British attack on the American frigate *Chesapeake* prompted Adams's support for Jefferson's foreign policy and led to his abandonment by his own Federalist party. However, Adams had long determined that his "sense of duty" should "never yield to the pleasure of a party" (1:469).

It was this decision to risk personal position for principle that established the dominant theme of both Adams's life and his diary, placing him as the isolated honest man battling for right in a selfish and evil world. This new role was so forcefully assumed that it prompted Adams to reconstruct his entire history in Congress according to its system. On October 30 he reviewed the journals of his days in the Senate and concluded that most of the work he had attempted had "failed with circumstances of peculiar mortification," while his successes were accomplished against irrationally "great obstinacy." Moreover, he found (or convinced himself that he had found) evidence that his own party had always treated him as a "subordinate member" and given him only "the merely laborious duties," and that his opinions had more frequently been "in unison with the administration than with their opponents" (1:471).

Convinced that his "moral and political principles" were "more pure" than those opponents who provoked him with "insidious and false imputations" (1:501) in Congress or who wrote "falsehoods and abuses" (1:516) in the newspapers, Adams prepared himself to accept the loss of his post. An example of this attitude is the entry for April 23, 1808, which not only offers an early statement of Adams's position in regard to public service but also, coincidentally, proved prophetic. To a friend's suggestion that he might take actions that would make him more politically acceptable as a candidate for a post such as that of secretary of state, Adams replied:

As to my being brought forward in a conspicuous station, I certainly did not think it a desirable thing. There was not a place in the gift of the people, or of the Executive of the United States, or of my own State, for which I had the slightest wish. That to be *dismissed* from the place which I now am in would doubtless occasion a moment of personal mortification, for which, however, my mind was made up, and which would be more than compensated by the advantage of being *released* from the cares of the public service at such a time as this; but that as to any thing else, so far as my personal desires were concerned, I would not speak ten words, nor write two lines, to be President of the United States—nor, of course, to be any thing subordinate to that. (1:533)

Consistent with these principles Adams resigned from the Senate rather than act in a manner more politically acceptable to his party and shortly afterward refused a call by the other party to be their candidate for that office.

Adams did accept the post of minister to the Russian government, but in the diary he expressed motives for and doubts about the acceptance:

It is with a deep sense of the stormy and dangerous career upon which I enter, of the heavy responsibility that will press upon it, and of the unpromising prospect which it presents in perspective. My personal motives for staying at home are of the strongest kind: the age of my parents and the infancy of my children both urge to the same result. . . . To oppose all this, I have the duty of a citizen to obey the call of his country signified by the regular constituted authority; the satisfaction of being removed, at least for a time, and with honor, from a situation where the deepest retirement has not sheltered me from the most virulent and unrelenting persecution; and the vague hope of rendering to my country some important service. (1:549)

The section covering Adams's mission to Russia and his subsequent post as head of the mission to make peace with Britain after the War of 1812 is among the best diplomatic diary material ever written. It begins with one of Adams's own poems (several are included in the diary), which invokes God for aid in his actions and suggests that the role of the diary was to ensure that Adams's thoughts as well as actions would be sufficiently worthy to make the book an exemplum on virtue:

> Eternal Spirit! Ruler of the skies!
> From whom all good and perfect gifts arise,
> Oh! grant that while this feeble hand portrays
> The fleeting image of my earthly days,
> Still the firm purpose of my heart may be
> Good to mankind, and gratitude to thee!
> And while the page a true resemblance bears
> Of all my changes through a life of cares,
> Let not one worthless deed here claim a place,
> To stain the future, or the past disgrace,
> Nor yet one thought the faithful record swell
> But such as virtue may delight to tell.
>
> (2:3)

If such a goal seems too grand, consider Adams's actual accomplishments.

Once out of sight of land on his voyage to Russia, Adams used the diary to tie together his past, represented by earlier voyages he had made to Europe with his father, with his present and future, expressed by this voyage and his coming mission. This process helped to prepare him for the work before him. Even the journey required Adams to show his skill in negotiation. When his ship was stopped by the British blockade, Adams proved as skillful as he would be in more elegant diplomatic encounters. Within weeks of landing, he was having a private audience with the Russian emperors and attending elegant balls and ceremonies.

In relating all these activities Adams showed a talent for describing in detail the physical appearances, events, and conversations that give his account the attractiveness of a novel. His "plot" is enhanced by the excitement of that particular place and time. The major historical event recorded in the diary of this mission was Napoleon's invasion of and subsequent retreat from Russia. Adams's description of the war is interestingly written; and, though his information about the actual battles was secondhand, his portrait of the response of the Russian court to the news such as the burning of Moscow was primary. The diary was not intended as a history of the Napoleonic wars, but rather of Adams's life in those times. In that context we can appreciate a remark in confidence that Napoleon suffered from gallstones (2:93), a chat with the Russian emperor on the virtues of flannel underwear (2:345), or an anecdote about how the newsboys hawking the latest bulletins found it easier to sell those dealing with Russian victories than those telling of Russian defeats (2:435–36).

As the excitement of war in Russia died down, Adams found himself once again moving to the center of action as chief of a mission to negotiate the end of the War of 1812. In this function he was joined by other American commissioners—James Bayard, Henry Clay, Albert Gallatin, and Jonathan Russell.[4] The disagreements, which were as marked between members of the American group as between that group and their British counterparts, offered a special opportunity for Adams to demonstrate his talent for characterization. Of course, in characterizing others he further developed his own self-portrait. For example, those entries in which Adams, rising a half hour before dawn to begin his work, heard Clay and his friends going to bed after a night of gambling say as much about the diarist as about his associates.

Such differences in temperament aggravated political friction between these men. In one entry Adams wrote, "Mr. Clay is losing his temper and growing peevish and fractious. I, too, must not forget to keep a constant guard upon my temper, for the time is evidently approaching when it will be wanted" (3:61). Two months later Adams recorded the following argument when Clay and two commissioners tried to take action without even consulting Adams:

I said . . . "The paper I had received was not an act of the majority, it was the act of three members."

"And although," said Mr. Clay, "those three members form a majority."

"Certainly," said I; "an act of greater number without consulting the other members is not an act of the majority."

Clay now lost all the remnant of his temper, and broke out with, "You dare not, you cannot, you SHALL not insinuate that there has been a cabal of three members against you; no person shall impute anything of the kind to me with impunity." . . . I replied, "What I dare say, I have dared to say in writing. Gentlemen may draw from it what inferences they please." (3:142–43)

Such political alliances and intrigues formed the plot of the diary almost from the beginning of negotiations until the peace was concluded.

Toward the end of 1816 oblique hints, rumors in newspapers, and secondhand accounts made it seem probable that Adams would be recalled to serve as secretary of state to President Monroe. Yet Adams tried to play down that possibility, questioning his own worthiness for the appointment and asserting that even if he deserved the post he should take no action to obtain it. The entry betrays his inner ambivalence. Believing, as his father did, that in a moral system desert required reward, Adams realized that if he were to become convinced that he merited the post, he risked not only personal disappointment, but also his faith in the political system he had so long worked to support. Thus, in the diary he manufactured doubts as to whether he was "fitted to discharge the heavy and laborious duties of the office" (3:458).

Four months later Adams received confirmation of his appointment and promptly made plans to return to America. By returning, Adams moved an important step closer to involvement in partisan politics. Landing in America, he resorted to his diary to record an awareness of the problems that were to come and his confidence that the God who had seen him through earlier difficulties would continue to aid him (4:3–4).

As his self-portrait in the diary reveals, Adams was able to banish both personal anxiety and political concerns in an attempt to surmount the problems of his new office. The entries about his first years as secretary of state, in turn, though fraught with information of great historical importance, present Adams's activities in so objective a manner that as either a personal or a literary document this section is one of the least viable of all those in the diary. Some entries have such a studied impartiality that potentially exciting scenes are flat and stiff. As a result, one of the most productive periods of Adams's life in terms of his service to his country is less interesting as a personal document than those formed from less politically significant portions of his career.

It was during this period that Adams negotiated the acquisition of Florida (which at the time Adams called "the most important event in my life") and helped to formulate the Monroe Doctrine. Adams repeatedly confided to the diary his belief that the Florida treaty was valuable not only because of the acquisition of Florida itself, but also because in defining the western boundary of the Louisiana Purchase it acknowledged America's claim to the land bordering the Pacific Ocean. In the long and intricate negotiations to secure this treaty Adams had to combat "the workings of private interests, of perfidious fraud or sordid intrigues or royal treachery, of malignance, and of envy masked with patriotism." All of his efforts and the "workings and windings" of other diplomats and politicians are recorded in the diary (4:305). Among the most interesting parts are those that record a dispute between Adams and the British ambassador. The following excerpts are only part of the material in those entries:

Mr. Canning, the British Minister called at the office, and intimating that he came to have some conversation with me in his official character . . . [inquired about the plans of some congressmen regarding an American] settlement on the Pacific Ocean. . . . The personal communications between Mr. Canning and me hitherto had all been of a character so conciliatory and friendly that, although much surprised both at the form and substance of this address, I answered him . . . that I was not acquainted with the opinions of those members of Congress on this subject, but, from a prevailing disposition in the country, it was very probable that our settlement at the mouth of Columbia River would at no remote period be increased.

He immediately assumed an air widely different from that of the easy familiarity with which the conversation had commenced, and, with a tone more peremptory than I was disposed to endure, said he was greatly surprised at receiving this answer. With a corresponding change of tone, I told him he could not be more surprised than I was, both at the form and substance of his address on this occasion.

"And am I to understand this," said he, "as the determination of the American Government?"

"No sir," said I; "you are to understand nothing as the determination of the American Government that I say to you without consultation and directions from the President. What I have said to you is merely an opinion of my own." (5:243–44)

As the discussion continued, Canning's temper and language became more heated, inflamed as much by Adams's condescending calmness as by the issues themselves. In one exchange Adams repeatedly tried to mention the cordial relationship that had existed between Mr. Bagot, the former British minister, and himself; however, Canning kept interrupting with words such as, "'I stop you there I will not endure a misrepresentation of what I say. . . .'" Then after a pause of a few moments he added, in the same passionate manner, 'I am treated like a schoolboy'" (5:246).

After several more exchanges the conversation was halted until the next day, at which point the dispute resumed. In exchanges such as the following Adams's irritation shows as his tone becomes more overly satiric:

"Have you any claim," said I, "to the mouth of Columbia River?"

"Why do you not know," replied he, "that we have a claim?"

"I do not know," said I, "what you claim nor what you do not claim. You claim India; you claim Africa; you claim—"

"Perhaps," said he, "a piece of the moon."

"No," said I; "I have not heard that you claim exclusively any part of the moon; but there is not a spot on this habitable globe that I could affirm you do not claim; and there is none which you may not claim with as much color of right as you can have to Columbia River or its mouth." (5:252)

This conversation with its passionate interchanges and subtle, yet evident manipulations of tone continues for many pages. Adams notes in the diary: "This narrative of two successive conversations with Mr. Canning is copied from a report of them which I committed to writing immediately after they occurred, my diary being then nearly three months in arrear" (5:259). The information about Adams's journalizing helps not only to account for the quality of those entries, but also to explain the relatively inferior quality of the diaries during his time as secretary of state and president, when his duties reduced the time available for diary keeping.

Another time in which personal involvement added notably to the vitality of the diary was the period surrounding Adams's election to the presidency. Early in the campaign Adams wrote:

We know so little of that in futurity which is best for ourselves, that whether I ought to wish for success is among the greatest uncertainties of the election. Were it possible to look with philosophical indifference to the event, that is the temper of mind to which I should aspire; but

> "Who can hold a fire in his hand
> By thinking on the frosty Caucasus?"

To suffer without feeling is not in human nature; and when I consider that to me alone, of all the candidates before the nation, failure of success would be equivalent to a vote of censure by the nation upon my past service, I cannot dissemble to myself that I have more at stake upon the result than any other individual in the Union. Yet a man qualified for the elective Chief Magistracy of ten millions of people should be a man proof alike to prosperous and to adverse fortune. If I am able to bear success, I must be tempered to endure defeat. He who is equal to the task of serving a nation as her chief ruler must possess resources of a power to serve her even against her own will. This is the principle that I would impress indelibly upon my own mind, and for the practical realization of which in its proper result I look to wisdom and strength from above. (6:323–24)

The election as Adams portrayed it in the diary was to be a personal test in which losing would assure failure, while winning promised no success. One biographer has labeled a chapter on the last two years of Adams's term as chief executive "The Tragic Presidency" because Adams faced both a hostile legislature and the growing likelihood of political defeat. Yet the diary shows that Adams viewed such opposition as evident and unavoidable before he was ever elected. On hearing word that his election seemed certain, Adams still expressed his conviction that "the real crisis" would come as the result of a "counter-movement" which would "be decisive the other way." While these lines seem directed to a set of political alliances that would work against his election, they suggest his awareness of the forces that would continue to work against him, making his "situation . . . difficult and trying beyond my powers of expression" (6:478–79). Historians and political scientists may direct their attention to Adams's political principles and his relation to the growing power of Jacksonian democracy, but readers concerned with his diary as a "personal and literary document" will find greater significance in his sense of being fated to be the victim of his own morality. This conviction, which is vitally related to earlier decisions such as giving up his seat in the Senate and not actively seeking the position of secretary of state, also proves important in explaining events recounted later in the diary.

The diary is full of instances of Adams's choice of principle over political advantage. Among the earliest of such decisions is the following:

I had been urged very earnestly, and from various quarters, to sweep away my opponents and provide places for my friends. I can justify the refusal to adopt this policy only by the steadiness and consistency of my adhesion to my own. If I depart from this in one instance, I shall be called upon by my friends to do the same in many. An invidious and inquisitorial scrutiny into the personal dispositions of officers will creep through the whole Union, and the most selfish and sordid passions will be kindled into activity to distort the conduct and misrepresent the feelings of men whose places may become the prize of slander upon them. (6:547)

As a result of such an attitude, Adams spent his presidency heading a bureaucracy that included large numbers of his political opponents, who used their positions to help turn the country away from him. Given Adams's view of defeat, a reader can readily understand how living in the growing shadow of the coming election would make this section of the diary tragic.

In 1830, two years after the failure of his campaign for reelection, John Quincy Adams had already served his country for over a third of a century and held the highest post in its government. At sixty-three he might have enjoyed a quiet retirement, but instead he stood for election to the House of Representatives and served there for nearly seventeen years. By 1830 his diary already encompassed about half a century and about two million words. One might expect that it too would lessen or lapse; but, like the political career of its author, a full third of the diary was yet to be written. Similarly, one might expect that, stripped of the individual power and unique position that he had enjoyed as minister, secretary of state, and president and made only one of hundreds of representatives, Adams's life would cease to be so interesting; but it was just this diminution of status and power that allowed him to become the political and literary hero he could never have been while he held the powers of the presidency.

The diary itself benefited from this shift in status by becoming more personal. No longer self-consciously the record of an administration, the diary like its major character had a greater opportunity to concern itself with the personal and the individual. This is not to say that Adams refrained from considering the background actions of his fellow congressmen. The diary became almost overloaded with minor characters from the Washington scene. But, while it is almost impossible without some record sheet to keep track of the mass of characters who popped in and out of the diary, the reader can quickly learn to merge all but a few into either the mass of opponents or the small group of supporters. To readers with a special knowledge or interest in the period these details can be mastered; but, for most, the sense of the section will be the merging of the political processes of the Congress, in which the hostile and friendly voices blend into a chorus against whose background Adams's melodies were sung.

Adams's diary shows the ambivalence with which he accepted his election. Not only did his age and health argue against it, but his own distaste for the intensely political nature of public service in Jacksonian America worked to dissuade him. The image that he conjured up in the diary to describe his new situation was one of being "launched again upon the faithless wave of politics" and "drifted . . . back again amidst the breakers of the political ocean" (8:243, 245). Another negative aspect of his election was that his friends and family disapproved of his "return to life in a subordinate station" (8:346). Several entries reveal that Adams felt it necessary to reiterate his position that he would do nothing to seek the post of representative but would consider as an honor any public service required by popular will. Adams declared that to reject the post because he had once been president would leave him subject to a charge of arrogance.

These factors were not the only ones that bore on Adams's final decision. Ten years earlier he had written in the diary:

In the continual bustle and unceasing occupation of my present office, I feel nothing but the want of time. But in looking forward to the moment when, discarded from all public concerns, my time will be all upon my hands, and, instead of the rapid whirl of successive stimulants to interest, the lifeless languor of indifference to everything around me will be predominant, what I principally dread is a dejection of spirits and atrophy of mind, which will throw me into a desultory and idle, because useless, career of reading indolence. (5:139)

Still more subtly but just as clearly expressed in the diary is Adams's search for signs of popular acceptance. Far from his public pose that he was intellectually and emotionally beyond discomfort from his defeat by Jackson in 1828, Adams confided in the diary his need for such an "unexpected testimonial of . . . continued confidence" as his election to the House" (8:246). The loss of public respect had been more crushing than the loss of position or power. Blows such as his nonreelection as president of the American Academy of Sciences, a post he had held ever since its formation, were sources of great anguish which could be forgotten thanks to this new "honor." Thus Adams could write: "My election as President of the United States was not half so gratifying in my soul" (8:247).

Once in Congress, Adams promptly moved to the center of controversy. He had long been concerned about slavery. In entries reminiscent of some in his father's diary he had condemned slavery not only for its degradation of the slave, but also for its debasement of the moral principles of the slave owner. He was particularly appalled at the way the supporters of slavery would divorce practice and principle, admitting in the abstract that slavery was wrong but insisting that in the South it was a benign system. After an argument with John Calhoun he complained in the diary:

It is among the evils of slavery that it taints the very sources of moral principle. It establishes false estimates of virtue and vice; for what can be more false and heartless than this doctrine which makes the first and holiest rights of humanity to depend upon the color of skin? It perverts human reason, and reduces man endowed with logical powers to maintain that slavery is sanctioned by the Christian religion, that slaves are happy and contented in their condition. (5:10–11)

Adams soon began to question his original decision to support the extension of slavery permitted by the Missouri Compromise as a means to preserve the Union, finally concluding: "If the Union must be dissolved, slavery is precisely the question on which it ought to break" (5:12).

Shortly after entering Congress, Adams found that in opposing slavery he would have to risk what remained of his political power and personal reputation. Even in his own district the abolition question forced him to "walk on the edge of a precipice in every step I take" (9:365). One of the steps that Adams took was the presentation of countless petitions against slavery and the slave trade. When the House passed the "gag rule," a regulation prohibiting the reception, printing, or discussion of petitions relating to slavery or the slave trade, Adams made the rescinding of this rule one of his major objectives. The effort took almost ten years.

In the meantime the diary recorded his stubborn persistence and "cutting sarcasm" (9:225). When the gag rule was passed, he recorded the following action on the floor of Congress:

> When my name was called, I answered, "I hold the resolution to be a violation of the Constitution, of the right of petition of my constituents, and of the people of the United States, and of my right to freedom of speech as a member of this House."
> I said this amidst a perfect war-whoop of order. (9:454)

It is the term "war whoop" that effectively labels as wild the attempt of his opponents to silence him. And thus, as the entry traces the parliamentary maneuvers to have his response entered in the record, Adams emerges as the lone civilized man battling the crude and un-principled savagery of unprincipled politicians:

> When I look upon the composition of these bodies, the Senate and the House of Representatives of the United States—the cream of the land, the culled darlings of fifteen millions, scattered over the surface of two millions of square miles—the remarkable phenomena that they present is the level of intellect and of morals upon which they stand; and this universal mediocrity is the basis upon which the liberties of this nation repose. (10:78–79)

Adams watched and recorded the slanders of "scoundrel" and "pup-py" (10:407), the threats of physical assaults and duels, and even the ridicule of a "half tipsy" adversary on the floor of the House itself (10:205). Yet his response was regret rather than anger. It is in this role as the civilized man fighting with his intellect and language that Adams appears in the following exchange about the admission of Texas to the Union: "I took the occasion, while up, of answering Waddy Thompson's declaration that he would vote for no new Northern Ter-ritory while Northern fanatics were pouring in petitions against the annexation to this Union of the great and glorious republic of Texas. I objected to the peculiar glory of Texas, which consisted of having made a land of free men a land of slaves. I said we had too much of that sort of glory already" (10:11).

In this setting Adams emerged wielding the stab of denunciation and the sting of epithet. A political enemy like Calhoun was labeled "high priest of Moloch, the embodied spirit of slavery"; and those Northern congressmen who, while claiming to "abhor slavery," helped to "forge fetters for the slave" by refusing to risk standing with him, were declared "political sopranos" (11:284–85). Disgusted by such a combination, he refused to go to the ceremony marking the construction of the Bunker Hill monument, writing in the diary:

With the ideal association of the thundering cannon, which I heard, and the smoke of burning Charlestown, which I saw, on that awful day, combined with this pyramid of Quincy granite, and Daniel Webster spouting, and John Tyler's nose, with a shadow outstretching that of the monumental column—how could I have witnessed all this at once, without an unbecoming burst of indignation, or of laughter? Daniel Webster is a heartless traitor to the cause of human freedom; John Tyler is a slave-monger. What have these to do with the Quincy granite pyramid on the brow of Bunker's Hill? What have these to do with a dinner in Faneuil Hall, but to swill like swine, and grunt about the rights of man? (11:383–84)

Adams did more than grunt. He went before the Supreme Court to argue successfully for the freedom of the Amistad captives, blacks illegally enslaved in Cuba who had seized possession of a ship and attempted to sail it to Africa. And he continued to make himself obnoxious by attempting to present antislavery petitions in defiance of the gag rule.

For one of these attempts Adams was brought to within a few votes of congressional censure and political disgrace. The petition that caused this problem asked that, because the nation as constituted could not abolish slavery, the Union be dissolved. Neither side appeared primarily concerned with the suggestion of dissolution. For Adams it was an oblique means to get around the gag rule and discuss abolition; for his opponents it was an opportunity to stifle the abolition movement by bringing Adams into disgrace. The diary treats the drama as a "fiery ordeal" (10:180) in which Adams described and answered threats of assassination and "personal invective" with eloquence and wit (11:76–83). He accepted the possibility of losing the very thing he valued most, his good name, so that his "opinions concerning the great movement throughout the civilized world for the abolition of slavery should be explicitly avowed and declared . . . [and so] contribute to the final consummation of the event" (11:406).

Adams did not live to see the success of abolition, but he did live to see both a growth in the movement and resurrection of his political popularity. On two trips west in 1843 Adams was, to his great surprise, "received by shouting multitudes" (11:396). Hailed by torchlight processions and begged for speeches, Adams confided his astonishment to his diary:

I then passed into the house, between a dense mass of population on both sides, but, as there was no general shaking of hands, as usual, immediately after the address, I was beset the whole evening by a succession of visitors in squads, to be introduced and shake hands, to every one of whom I was a total stranger, and the name of not one of whom can I remember. My friends . . . give me every possible aid and encouragement in getting along; but the strangeness of these proceedings increases like a ball of snow. I cannot realize that these demonstrations are made for me; and the only comfort I have is that they are intended to manifest respect, and not hatred. (11:423)

Reelected to Congress in 1844 despite great opposition, Adams declared it was "a result which I dared not expect and upon which I dare not attempt to express my feelings" (12:106). On returning to the House of Representatives he gave notice of his determination to move that the gag rule be rescinded. At last, after praising God for the victory, he was able to write in the diary that his quest was successful. As a symbol of his victory he accepted an ivory cane topped with "a golden eagle bearing a scroll with the motto 'Right of Petition Triumphant'" (12:182).

Another important theme in Adams's diaries began during these years of service as a member of the House of Representatives and came to dominate the diary: his growing concern with religion, aging, and death, subjects that were all but ignored in the earlier sections. Men seem to turn naturally to such topics as they grow old, and so this development is not surprising; but, as age tends to diminish the energy men have available, this event is rarely so fully developed in diaries. Adams's habit of diary keeping was so firmly established that he continued it even after physical disability made recording a struggle (11:542).

Some hints of this area of concern appear a little earlier in the diary. For example, when Adams, who was almost sixty himself, attended the marriage of two friends, he wrote:

The parties are each about three score years of age. . . . The couple thus
united cannot have many years to live together. Their contemporaries, blooming in youth as I had seen them all, are now, some bending under the weight
of years, and faces where I had seen roses in bloom were now furrowed, wrin-
kled, and haggard. I, too, have gone through a corresponding change, and
was an object of meditation to them, as they were to me. Cupid and Hymen!
what worshippers of yours are these! (8:244–45)

The association of his own situation with that of the newlyweds is an
indication that Adams recognized that, despite his care to maintain his
physical strength, he must grow old.

Soon the diary had a new aspect. A work designed to record the
present for the future became in part a theater for the recollection of
the past. The anniversary of the signing of the Treaty of Ghent made
him remember not only his early fears of failure and unexpected success, but also the passing of many of the participants of that conference
(9:3–4). Another anniversary, that of his return from France in 1779,
prompted him to recall:

How many scenes of good and of evil fortune have I since passed! How many
of deep distress! how many of exquisite enjoyment! how many of severe trial!
how many of painful and pleasant labor! how many of overruling passion! and
how few of virtuous self-denial and of disinterested exertion for the good of
my fellow-creatures! I cannot say, like Rousseau of Geneva, that I am prepared
to present myself before the throne of Omnipotence with my confessions in
my hand, and affirm that no better man than myself ever lived. There have
been better, because there have been incomparably wiser men. I have little to
answer for in my relations with mankind, and have a firm though humble
reliance on the mercy of my Maker. A return of rheumatic infirmity this day
gave me a new admonition to prepare for the close of life. (9:12)

The last sentence is not totally a non sequitur—it sprang naturally out
of the backward vision.

As these memories occurred, his own failing physical condition became apparent, and Adams had to console himself with spiritual sat-
isfactions. Even his sleep suffered so that instead of "seven hours of
peaceful slumber," he slept no more than five, and that brief period
was "always disturbed, unquiet sleep—full of tossings." However,
though his sleep was troubled, he could take comfort in his conviction
that unlike so many other men he, at least, still possessed a clear con-

science which kept him from "the misery of rising with self-reproach" (9:28).

In such a state many events directed his thought to musings upon "the frailty of human life" (9:92). Among these was the death on the floor of the House of a fellow congressman, a death that, unknown to Adams, prefigured his own. To the knowledgeable reader such coincidences give Adams's diary a greater sense of artistic unity than might have been intentionally created.

In this mood Adams turned to religion, declaring the "promise of the scriptures" a source of pleasure and the Emersonian "doctrine of transcendentalism" a threat not only to religion, but also to the very "cornerstones of human society" (10:275, 350). In old age these became serious concerns for a man who had not formally become a member of a church until after the death of his father, when he himself was already in his late fifties. Coming at the age of seventy-five, statements such as the following do more to argue that Adams's focus had shifted than that his faith had been constant:

I have at all times been a sincere believer in the existence of a Supreme Creator of the world, or an immortal principle within myself, responsible to that Creator for my conduct upon earth, and of the divine mission of the crucified Saviour, proclaiming immortal life and preaching peace on earth, good will to men, the natural equality of all mankind, and the law, "Thou shalt love thy neighbor as thyself." Of all these articles of faith, all resting upon the first, the existence of an Omnipotent Spirit, I entertain involuntary and agonizing doubts, which I can neither silence nor expel, and against which I need for my own comfort to be fortified and sustained by stated and frequent opportunities of receiving religious admonition and instruction. I feel myself to be a frequent sinner before God, and I need to be often admonished of it, and exhorted to virtue. (11:341)

His emotional state is clearly revealed in the following entry:

My mind is in the condition of a ship at sea in a hurricane, suspended by an instantaneous calm. The brain heaves, the head swims, the body totters, and I live in a perpetual waltz. The presentiment of a sudden termination to my life is rather cheering to me than painful, and a man conscious of no sin upon his soul which repentant tears may wash out can dispense with the deprecation of the Episcopal litany against sudden death. The apprehension, however, of such a close to my life ought to and does admonish me to set my house in order to be prepared as much as a prudent forecast can provide for whatever event may by the will of God befall me. . . . The mercy of God is the only anchor of my soul for deliverance from this ordeal. (11:247)

The extent to which Adams succeeded in setting his house in order will be judged differently by those who accept his own opinion measured against his high personal standards and those who measure his achievements against those of most men. In August 1846 the first session of the 29th Congress ended and Adams returned home. From this point on, the diary entries are fragmentary, but they give us a picture of his emotional state. In one entry he wrote:

Blessing, praise, and supplication to God on first rising from bed on returning to my earthly home, after an absence of nine months in the public service of my country. Some discouragement of soul follows the reflection that my aspirations to live in the memory of after-ages as a benefactor of my country and of mankind have not received the sanction of my Maker; that the longing of my soul through a long life to be numbered among the blessings bestowed by the Creator on the race of man is rejected; and after being trammeled and counteracted and disabled at every step of my progress, my faculties are now declining from day to day into mere helpless impotence. Yet at the will of my heavenly Father why should I repine? (12:271)

Finally in November of 1846, Adams suffered a stroke. Upon recovery, he entered the following account in his diary:

On Friday, the 20th November, 1846, being at my son's house, in Mount Vernon Street, Boston . . . I attempted to walk out with Dr. George Parkman . . . [but] I suddenly found myself unable to walk, and my knees sinking under me. . . . I was put to bed, to which I was several days and nights confined, with a suspension of bodily powers, with little or no pain and little exercise of intellect. From that hour I date my decease, and consider myself, for every useful purpose to myself or to my fellow-creatures, dead; and hence I call this and what I may write hereafter a posthumous memoir. (12:279)

But Adams did survive. A year after his stroke he returned to Washington, where, on February 21, he was stricken on the floor of Congress. He was carried to a chamber in the House, where he died the next day.

In one of his last diary entries Adams offered a great tribute to the diary form, suggesting that the ultimate diary of a life could be the greatest literary work. Those devoted to the genre could hardly ask for a stronger endorsement; nor, I believe, would they find Adams's diary falling as short of their ideal as he himself implied:

There has perhaps not been another individual of the human race, of whose daily existence from early childhood to fourscore years has been noted down with his own hand so minutely as mine. At little more than twelve years of age I began to journalize. . . . If my intellectual powers had been such as have been sometimes committed by the Creator of man to single individuals of the species, my diary would have been, next to the Holy Scriptures, the most precious and valuable book ever written by human hands, and I should have been one of the greatest benefactors of my country and of mankind. I would, by the irresistible power of genius and the irrepressible energy of will and the favor of Almighty God, have banished war and slavery from the face of the earth forever. But the conceptive power of mind was not conferred upon me by my Maker, and I have not improved the scanty portion of His gifts as I might and ought to have done. (12:276–77)

This passage reveals Adams's humanistic faith in the power of ideas, a power weakly valued in this modern age. This view prefigured the conclusion that John Quincy's grandson, Henry Adams, would assert in his own autobiography, that a symbol could be a potent historical force and that a work of art could be the means for expressing or directing that force. Adams's diary is a true "life diary" giving a full account of a full life. His last words are not part of the diary proper, but they form a fitting conclusion to it: "This is the last of earth; I am content."

Multigeneration Diaries

John Quincy Adams's diary was only one of a series of diaries kept by members of his family over several generations. This inheritance of the practice of diary keeping was not unique; however, the diaries of the Adams family probably form the finest example of a multigeneration diary. John Quincy Adams adopted his practice from his father and mother and passed it on to his wife and children. In considering such diaries one should be aware that frequently the actual diaries were passed on, with the habit contributing to the diarists' expectations that their works would be open to view. For example, John Quincy Adams wrote in his diary of spending an afternoon in his father's library "much entertained in reading some journals of my father's" (*L*, 55). In the next generation Charles Francis Adams edited both his father's and his grandfather's diaries, activities which could not have helped but influence his own work.

Among John Quincy Adams's sons, only Charles Francis Adams kept a diary that is worthy of major consideration as a literary work; however, since over half of it, including the most important events in its author's career, was written in the last half of the nineteenth century, I have chosen to reserve that consideration for another study.

John Quincy Adams's wife, Louisa Catherine Adams, kept a diary with some interesting sections, but her habit was sporadic. In her first entry (October 12, 1812) she explained that she had begun the work not just to record her thoughts, but also "to avoid dwelling on the secret and bitter reproach of my heart for my conduct as it regarded my Lost adored Child whose death was surely occasion'd by procrastination."[5] The diary continued to be used at times of stress, especially those occasioned by family illnesses or political controversies. A good example is the following entry dated December 14, 1835:

How bitterly sick I am of all the nefarious details of political life. Condemnations would be passed upon me generally for my opinions, but when the grave yawns before us we see with different eyes and the tinsel and glitter of the world palls upon the mind, the basest characters; the most disgusting mess; the basest intrigues; the most unblushing lies; the most malignant misrepresentations, backbiting, slander, and all the fabrications of the lowest and most venial minds; perpetually goaded by the worst passions form its basis. . . . Even the hearts of the most honest men must be kindled into a rage by the consistent unshrinking malevolence of party spirit.

Even though its fragmentary nature keeps Louisa Catherine Adams's diary from approaching the quality of those of her husband and her son Charles, it is interesting, and it does help to provide a special context for the works of other family members.

Chapter Six
Transcendentalist Journals

A definition of Transcendentalist journals seems simple. It is that body of diary literature written by proponents of Transcendentalism in accordance with the worldview derived from that system of belief. Unfortunately, there is no general agreement on a definition of Transcendentalism, and there has never been such agreement. In his story "The Celestial Railroad" Hawthorne satirized Transcendentalism by portraying it as a "terrible giant" whose "form" and substance were so indistinct "that neither he for himself, nor anybody for him has ever been able to describe them." Emerson in his essay "The Transcendentalist" defined Transcendentalism as "Idealism," a belief that the world is made up of ideas, not matter, and that the world of the senses only represents the real world of the spirit. Yet this basic belief fails to include the fact that Transcendentalism also involved a method of perceiving and using that spiritual *reality*. The goal of a Transcendentalist was to transcend, to go beyond physical appearance either by using intuition and mysticism to *see* truth directly or by learning the symbolic language by which spiritual truth could be read in its physical manifestations.

The attempts of Transcendentalists to learn and follow the lessons of the spirit were similar to those of proponents of more traditional religious systems to learn and follow God's plan. As a result, the function of the journals of the Transcendentalists was very similar to that shared by many spiritual diarists. Indeed, the journals of Transcendentalists such as Emerson are descendants of Puritan spiritual journals just as many of the Transcendentalists were descendants of the Puritans.

In colonial society traditional religious forms dominated the life of the mind. In the early nineteenth century the variety and independence of spiritual activity increased. The diaries of the Transcendentalists are very much concerned with the spirit, but, just as those diarists had a less-focused and specific conception of God than did writers of what has been termed the spiritual diary, so their diaries included a broader range of concerns. Another point of comparison between the traditional spiritual journal and the form written by the Transcendentalists is that the authors of both classes of journal sought to find evidence of their place in the divine scheme either directly through religious experience or indirectly through finding a pattern in the world God had created. Just as many Puritans hoped to use the perceptions and patterns found through their journalizing to demonstrate God's intentions, including their own salvation, so many Transcendentalists kept diaries to demonstrate their spiritual perceptions.

However, while many of the Transcendentalists explored those perceptions in their journals, spiritual perceptions constituted only one part of their journal material. And, more significantly, their journalizing was more concerned with the process of discovery than with the truth discovered. Just as the young Emerson may have been less attracted to the Harvard Divinity School as an opportunity to study religion than as a "chance to pursue his career as Man Thinking," so in developing his journal he seems to have been more concerned with its effect on his thinking and writing than with its particular revelations.[1]

The multiple motives of the best diarists among the American Transcendentalists suggest that many of their works, and certainly the ones covered in this chapter, are more appropriately classed as life diaries than as variations of either the traditional spiritual journal or the literary notebook. The assignment of subgeneric categories is much easier when one is dealing with those serial records that focus on physical events rather than those that primarily treat spiritual concerns. It is always easier to categorize objects and events than mental or spiritual concepts.

Emerson and many of the other diarists among the American Transcendentalists used their diaries as a means of improving their writing and as a sourcebook that might be mined for materials to be used in their public writings. In this sense their diaries were very much literary notebooks; indeed, several of the Transcendentalists came to recognize that their raw journals were, themselves, literary works.

The best of the diaries kept by the American Transcendentalists during this period are those of Emerson, Alcott, and Thoreau.[2] Margaret Fuller's journal may well have been worthy of inclusion; however, in editing their *Memoirs of Margaret Fuller Ossoli,* Emerson, Channing, and Clarke mutilated or lost so much of that work that too little survives.

Ralph Waldo Emerson (1803–1882)

On January 25, 1820, Ralph Waldo Emerson, then a junior at Harvard, began a series of diary entries entitled "The Wide World." Just as John Winthrop's decision to title a portion of his personal record *A History of New England* offers a helpful clue to understanding that work, so Emerson's choice of "The Wide World" as a title for his "commonplace book" is an aid to our understanding of this portion of his record. This title suggests that, at least initially, Emerson viewed his journals as an opening to the world rather than a means to retire into his own solitary speculations.

"The Wide World" was not Emerson's first attempt at journalizing, for he had already kept a series of notebooks containing first drafts of college essays, poems, and miscellaneous jottings. One of these notebooks, titled "College Theme Book," has entries dating back to 1819, and the earliest extant volume of the notebooks, dated 1820, was given the number XVII. This numbering suggests that Emerson's habit of journalizing had begun well before he entered college.

Notebook XVII begins with a draft essay Emerson was writing for the Bowdoin Prize contest. In it he wrote that, "in a money making community literature will soon thrive. It must always follow not precede successful trade. The first wants to be supplied are the native ones of animal subsistence & comfort & when these are more than provided for . . . the mind then urges its claim to cultivation."[3] Here Emerson seems prophetic. In suggesting that cultures first value those "commodities" that may be consumed or physically manipulated but, as they develop, increasingly value products of the mind and spirit, he seems not only to be exploring a concept that would become the structuring theme of *Nature,* but also to be predicting that the explosive growth of the American economy then underway would lead to the cultural explosion of the "American Renaissance." Moreover, this passage, along with other hints in the notebook, indicates the young man's hope for a market for his future writing. This interest in a literary career was even clearer in the "Wide World" journals.

Emerson's professed goals for his journals were the profit and entertainment that might be gained by "mixing with the thousand pursuits & passions & objects of the world as personified by the Imagination" (1:3–4). This intention to blend his own current thoughts with interesting information from the works of others not only reinforces this view of Emerson's early attitude toward his work, but also establishes a basis for his very loose definition of diary forms. Many diarists begin their works as informal, unrestricted jottings, but few diarists write works of any length or substance without accepting some formal restrictions. However, Emerson persisted in his practice of alternating, almost at random, between descriptions and perceptions of the external world typical of the subgenre I have termed "diary proper," generalized internal musings characteristic of the "journal" subgenre, and records of formal exercises directed toward publication. Even those diaries most likely to be compared to Emerson's, the journals of Thoreau and Alcott, are far more homogeneous.

Emerson's composition practices help to clarify his attitude toward the nature of the *Journals*. His pattern of composition and notebook use was often erratic. He occasionally departed from the page-to-page chronological sequence of most diaries. It appears that he not only added or altered earlier entries but also, often randomly, filled space previously left blank (1:xli). Such practices occasionally create problems for scholars, but, since Emerson's journals did not primarily deal with external events, they rarely cause problems for the general reader.

At least in their early entries, the "Wide World" journals were directed toward the fancy rather than the intellect. In expressing this division between the realms of imagination and reason the young Emerson seems to have been taking a position closer to that found in Poe's essays than in his own maturer writings. For example, in commenting on one lapse in journalizing he admitted that during that period he had been active in his thought and writing but that these items were not the type he intended for his journal. He implied that he conceived of a clear break between his serious studies and his inclination toward those works of magic and chivalry that "would let my soul sail away delighted in their wildest phantasies" (1:10–11). A few entries later he added that the journal "was intended to restore the sinking soul, to keep alive the fire of enthusiasm of literature, & literary things, to be the register of desultory but valuable contemplations" (1:15).

In his first entry Emerson invoked the supernatural aid of witches to "enliven or horrify some midnight lucubration or dream . . . to supply this reservoir when other resources fail," and he begged the pardon of "Fairy Land! rich region of fancy & gnomery, elvery and sylphery & Queen Mab!" for petitioning its enemies. He even called upon the "Spirits of earth, Air, Fire . . . [to] hallow this devoted paper" (1:4). In an entry only six weeks later, his memory faulty, Emerson apologized to the "Gnomes to whom I dedicated this quaint & heterogeneous manuscript" for a lapse in the diary (1:10). After a subsequent gap he suggested that "malignant demons" might have "possessed themselves of my mind & pen & my tongue & my book" (1:15). Emerson's delight in such romantic images of the supernatural continued in the poems, fables, and brief references that found expression in the later parts of his diary as well as in his other writings.[4]

The journals also had a more serious use as a means for directing their author's behavior. Emerson included resolutions to engage in or be more energetic in his studies and to avoid tendencies to be "idle, vagrant, stupid & hollow" (1:15, 39). He also used his journals for spiritual direction, a means to prompt withdrawal "from sin & the world the idle or vicious time & thoughts" and so prepare for his expected career in the ministry. Another implied function of his journalizing was the improvement of his writing skill (1:33). The young Emerson had high hopes for his writings but he mistrusted his ability: "What therefore is left, but for me to confide in the silent sheets of my book which cannot insult and will not betray" (1:60–61).

In his journals Emerson could not only experiment with his technique, but also express his strongest feelings. As the editors of the *Journals* have noted, though Emerson was considered outspoken in his public works, he "sometimes toned down or altered his original thought when he presented it for public consumption" (1:xxxii). This observation can be extended and adapted to apply to those passages of the *Journals* not published in another form. They too occasionally contain franker, more forceful, and more personally revealing statements than Emerson permitted himself to express publicly.

Certainly, Emerson felt that he had put his soul in his journals, admitting in one entry, "I must spin my thread from my bowels." So strong were his motives for journalizing that even when he felt that it would be "the prodigality of ink the wanton destruction of paper to add another syllable," he found himself compelled to write on (4:81). Still later in what seems a reflection on his own experience, he wrote: "Every young person writes a journal into which when the hours of prayer & penitence arrive he puts his soul. The pages which he has written in the rapt moods are to him burning & fragrant. He reads them by midnight & by the morning star he wets them" (8:123).

Emerson's personal references are rarely this clear. Because so many of his entries were couched as impersonal essays, the reader of the *Journals* will have a more difficult time in determining which ones contain statements that apply to their author than will the reader of most diaries. Consider Emerson's warning, "never mistake yourself to be great, or designed for greatness, because you have been visited by an indistinct and shadowy hope that something is reserved for you beyond the common lot. . . . The very idleness which leaves you leisure to dream of honor is the insurmountable obstacle between you and it" (1:100). Was he chiding his own tendency toward such visions? A careful reading of the journals will suggest other interpretations. For example, in one entry Emerson compared his earlier role as student to his present one as a "hopeless schoolmaster," arguing that his misery was his own fault, the result of building "castles in the air" (1:130). This entry gives the reader some license to interpret as autobiographical one following it that pretended to be an objective argument against the "Passions" (1:131).

In the early journals Emerson occasionally expressed views that diverged greatly from those in his later writings. In one entry he declared that the origin of evil was "the sin which Adam brought into the world and entailed upon his children" (1:93). In another passage he criticized following one's impulses, the very "whims" which he would extol in "Self-Reliance," by claiming man's ability to renounce the passionate impulse is what "distinguishes him from the beasts" (1:131). Emerson even downgraded the value of the "Solitude" he would later declare to be so important, suggesting that while a life spent in solitude might be "innocent," it could "hardly be greatly virtuous" (1:98). These early entries underscore the fact that his values were not yet fixed. For example, two days after writing the entry cited above he wrote another extolling the excitement of "A breathless solitude" (1:99).

When, at the beginning of "The Wide World No. 4," Emerson wrote of having previously "invoked successively the Muse, the fairies, the witches, and Wisdom . . . Imagination from within and Nature from without . . . [and even] Time," he had already begun to abandon such devices.[5] By October 1824, when he labeled his new volume "Journal No. XV," the "Wide World" heading itself was dropped (1:91). Like these dedications, the content of the journals began to show a gradual, although by no means uniform, movement toward more serious and practical subjects. Not only were there fewer poems and fables, but these become directed toward weightier topics. By the end of the "Wide World" journals Emerson's life had undergone significant changes, he had begun his professional studies and, turning twenty-one, was "*legally* a man" (2:237). But more significantly for students of his journals, his work had also come of age.

The first pages of the journals have both interest and eloquence, but not until encountering the entries written early in late 1822 or early 1823 will most readers detect a similarity between the language of Emerson's journals and that of his published essays. Yet, were Emerson's rhythmic cadences, agile alliterative devices, images, and questions born suddenly from the womb of "Wide World No. 10"? No! All experience calls upon us to affirm that the acquisition of style is ever gradual. One can go back and discover that the style has been building all along, but unless one is looking for it or is unusually astute, one will not detect it until the frequency of stylistic clues is sufficient. Then one will find lines like the following:

There is nothing in a fable so dark & dreadful but had its first model in the houses and palaces of men. (2:88–89)

A young man who is gathering up his bundle of experience counts many matters of old observation to be his own discoveries. (2:152)

If I am asked why the hope of heaven is thus broken—while the hopes of the lover the scholar and the statesman are active enough, I answer that their objects are tangible and require no farsighted sagacity to bring them home to the feelings. (2:166)

From this point on Emerson the diarist seems truly the same Emerson that readers are familiar with from the published works. For example, in the beginning of "Wide World No. 12" he wrote:

The world changes its masters, but keeps its own identity, and entails upon each new family of the human race, that come to garnish it with names & memorials of themselves,—certain indelible features and unchanging properties. Proud of their birth to a new & brilliant life, each presumptuous nation boasts its dominion over nature. . . . The world which they inhabit they call their servant, but it proves the real master. (2:187)

These lines seem to echo those of the poem "Hamatreya" (1846), with its farmers who think they own their land until they die and are added to it: "Earth laughs in flowers to see her boastful boys / Earth-proud, proud of the earth which is not theirs."

In October 1824, Emerson began "Journal No. XV," the first extant number without the "Wide World" heading. This period was the beginning of the second phase in his diary production. Among the inscriptions and quotations on the front cover of this number of the *Journals* Emerson included a modified quotation from Bacon to assert that he was the architect of his own fortunes.[6] While the previous spring he had written, "I am the servant more than the master of my fates" (2:245), in "Journal No. XV" he began to take responsibility for his fate, admitting that "Those men to whom the muse has vouchsafed her inspirations, fail, when they fail, by their own fault" (2:309).

Emerson's affirmation of this active ambition seems not to have extended to diary production. In the next eight years of his journal he did not even write as much as he had in the less than four years of the "Wide World." If one includes the writings in the miscellaneous notebooks, the discrepancy becomes even more pronounced. Part of this reduction in diary production may have occurred because Emerson devoted much of his time to his studies in the Divinity School and to the composition of sermons for his ministry;[7] however, his earlier and later journalizing suggest that this explanation offers only a partial answer.

Among the other factors that might explain Emerson's reduced diary production was his attitude toward the utility of such a journal. Although he had abandoned the romanticized content of some of the early journals, to a man determined to enter the ministry journalizing may have seemed less worthy than other activities. Emerson certainly seems to have been concerned about practical results when he wrote: "Infirmities are already stealing on me that may be the deadly enemies that are to dissolve me to dirt and little is yet done to establish my consideration among my contemporaries & less to get a memory when I am gone" (3/27/26).

Approximately halfway through this second phase of his diary production Emerson announced in his journal, "I have now been four days engaged to Ellen Louisa Tucker" (3:148–49). It was the first time her name appeared in the journal and one of only a few references made to her there until after her death on February 13, 1831. In one of these rare entries Emerson declared that this "angel" was the gift of God, which, coinciding with the call "by an ancient & respectable church to become its pastor," suggested a kind and protecting providence (3:149). When his "angel" proved mortal, his life and faith changed radically.

Five days after Ellen's death Emerson wrote that she had gone to heaven not only "to see, to know, to love [and] to worship," but also "to intercede." She would, he hoped, pray for him that he might be rid of "sins & selfishness," think "good thoughts" and see the truth. But, though a minister, he was not so confirmed in his faith to fasten on such hopes and so keep his life on its previous course. This same entry contains a mystical vision but not a hopeful one: "Two nights since, I have again heard her breathing, seen her dying." Emerson

seems almost to have been one of Poe's characters as he pleaded, "Re-
unite us, o thou Father of our Spirits," before finally concluding,
"There is that which passes away & never returns." When he asked,
"Will the . . . dead be restored to me? Will the eye that was closed on
Tuesday ever beam again in the fullness of love on me?" the *raven* voice
of his journal answered back, "No there is one birth & one baptism &
one first love and the affections cannot keep their youth any more than
men" (3:226–27). Convinced that if Ellen should forget him it would
be the death of his ambition, he persisted in his melancholy search for
her (3:228), even going so far as to visit her tomb and to open the
coffin (4:7). She was, he complained, "nowhere & yet everywhere"
(3:257). But though he begged that he might, at least, meet her "on
the midnight wing of dreams," he was forced to conclude that he could
never recapture that "vision . . . too beautiful to last" except through
"the welcome stroke" of death (3:230–31).

One result of Emerson's despair was a questioning of religious in-
tuitions. Using his diary in this process, he found his answer not in
the church with its public worship, but in the "awful solitudes in
which . . . a soul lives," and which are the environment for diary production (3:272). He studied "the art of solitude," and his meditations
suggested to him that the truth was to be found in nature and the soul
itself, not in minister and scripture (5:58). Concluding that the heart
taught the same truths as did Christ, Emerson asked himself, "why
then shall I not go to my own heart at first?" (4:45). He did not totally
discard his old religion but came to consider it as a lower stage of
development, like the tadpole or fetus, that would lead to a higher
stage. Christianity he termed a "temporary" device, a scaffolding,
which God had been employing "to educate man" but would "set
aside" when its work was completed (4:8). This development, which
Emerson would explore in his "Divinity School Address," would require that all men follow the example of Jesus in recognizing the divinity within themselves.

Emerson had long believed that a minister's function was "to show
the beauty of the moral laws of the universe; to explain the theory of a
perfect life; to watch the Divinity in his world; to detect his footstep;
to discern him in the history of the race of his children" (3:152). Now
with his new conception of the divine as both "the Soul at the center
by which all things are what they are" and a part of the soul within
man, Emerson began to find that many of the functions of the Unitar-
ian minister violated his own conscience (4:29, 33). By July 1832,

these beliefs were bringing him to his "hour of decision." Declaring that "Jesus did not mean to institute a perpetual celebration," Emerson decided to resign from the ministry (4:30).

A month after his final resignation Emerson, himself in ill health, suffered another tragedy, the death of his sister Margaret. He hoped that, free from her "painful corporeal imprisonment," Margaret might "rejoice with Ellen, so lately lost, in God's free and glorious universe," but he could see no such benefit for himself (4:60). He had only a very narrow circle of acquaintances, and thus, the loss of wife and sister left him very alone (4:62). In this despair Emerson's second period of diary production ended; his hopes for his ministry and family seemed ended, too—both were, at least, radically altered.

The next section of the *Journals* is essentially a travel diary. Emerson continued to write the philosophical speculations that prepared him for his later essays, but this portion of the work is richer in its description of external events than of transcendental perceptions. He made some notes in the copybook he had been using before the trip, but most of the travel section was recorded in separate notebooks reserved for this purpose.

On Christmas day, 1832, Emerson set sail for the Mediterranean.[8] His first entry tells of a storm at sea that not only made him seasick but also made him fear for his life. Even nature, which at other times could be so comforting, seemed reduced to "the ugly sound of water" (4:102–3). If before the storm Emerson had entertained the notion that the sea's "howling infinite" might purge his spirit of fear or melancholy, he did not record it in his diary. However, afterward he did affirm that "the mists & the wind & the sea" sang of God's power and that by acknowledging God the soul could realize that "the question whether your boat shall float in safety or go to the bottom is no more important than the flight of a snowflake" (4:103–4). Encountering a severe storm on his return voyage, Emerson wrote that though his ship swam "like a waterfowl betwixt the mountains of sea," he should not pray "for safety from danger but for deliverance from fear. . . . [and from] the storm within" (4:86).

On February 3, 1833, Emerson arrived in the harbor of Malta. Setting foot in Europe for the first time, he declared that his purpose in making this journey was "to find new affinities between me & my fellow men, to observe narrowly the affections, weaknesses, surprises, hopes, doubts, which new sides of the panorama shall call forth in me" (4:68). But this newness would not be only external, for he felt "so rude and unready" that every day seemed a new beginning (4:67).

Many of Emerson's descriptions of his experiences were typical tourist's notes—articulate descriptions, but without any special perceptual or philosophic framework; however, others suggest some patterns. For example, he seems to have been very affected by the recognition of connections that transcended time: "a crumbled arch reputed as the spot where Cicero found the globe & cylinder, the tomb of Archemedes"; ancient catacombs surrounded by wildflowers offering an argument that "amidst ruin of ruins Nature was still fair"; an "Aqueduct which once supplied the magnificent city of Hiero, now turning a small grist mill"; a Roman temple still "devoted to divine worship as a Christian church" (4:122, 124). Passing a monument to an ancient conqueror, Emerson mused, "Did he think that Mr. Emerson would be reminded of his existence & victory this spring day 2047 years to come?" (4:128–29). As he would later conclude in his poem "Each and All," Emerson began to realize that things might be connected in unforeseen ways.

Emerson seems to have been surprised by the difference between Italy and his native land, writing, "all, all is Italian; not a house, not a shed, not a field that the eye can for a moment imagine to be American" (4:177). Visiting Rome, he rhapsodized that it "fashions my dreams. All night I wander amidst statues & fountains, and last night was introduced to Lord Byron! It is a graceful termination to so much glory that Rome now in her fallen state should be the metropolis of the arts" (4:159). But upon seeing Florence, Emerson altered his opinion of Rome's artistic supremacy: "I think no man has an idea of the powers of painting until he has come hither. Why should painters study at Rome? Here, here" (4:168).

When he finally reached France he was already worn with wonders, and the account of his month in Paris is brief. His treatment of a month and a half in Britain is little longer, and most of it is contained in entries recounting his visits with Wordsworth, Coleridge, and Carlyle. The record of his encounter with the latter is fragmentary, but this fragmentation seems the result of Emerson's attempt to jot down notes that would later help him to recall important elements. As he was about to leave Europe he wrote: "I thank the great God who has led me through this European scene, this last schoolroom in which he has been pleased to instruct me . . . & now has brought me to the shore & to the ship that steers westward" (4:78).

The trip had had a profound effect on Emerson's ego; before, he had expressed his desire for great achievements as a distant hope; afterward, they seemed within his grasp. He had come into contact with the great men he had most wanted to see—Landor, Coleridge, Carlyle, and Wordsworth; and, while he still declared them "men of genius," he found none met his standards for "a mind of the very first class." This judgment was based on his conclusions that all had deficiencies, especially "in insight into religious [moral] truth" and that their conversation made "no deep impression." Indeed, Emerson declared that one of his school students had been "as wise a talker as . . . these men" (4:78–79).

Despite such comments, it would be a mistake to imagine that Emerson was seeking to debase these men whom he had found so "rich in thought," so "amiable"; rather, he had gained a greater respect for human capacity. It was the confident frankness of these men that had enabled them to rise above the common, and Emerson concluded that their example showed that many a self-reliant man might do as well. Certainly, he had come to believe that he himself might do as well and so should be less timid in the future (4:78–79).

Emerson's new confidence may seem extremely egotistical, but he had become aware of twin pitfalls, on one hand the danger of the want of self-reliance, the doubting of one's own potential; on the other, the dangers of flattery and egotism. Having seen that, impressed by great achievements, the public makes idols of those who have performed them, he declared that this "premature canonization" was as dangerous to those so flattered as to those who offered this adulation (4:79). Emerson had come to believe what he would later assert in "The American Scholar," that while "the act of creation" was sacred, there was little value in having created. The doing was all, and he returned home to America prepared to begin doing. By the time he began his voyage home, he was already at work on *Nature;* and, though he was not yet sure about how he ought to conduct his life, he had confidence that "God would show him" (4:237).

About three weeks after his return to America, Emerson preached at the church from which he had resigned the previous year, but he did not think of returning to the ministry. Three days earlier he had written in his journal: "The teacher of the coming age must occupy himself in the study & explanation of the moral constitution of man more than the elucidation of difficult texts. He must work in the conviction that the scripture can only be interpreted by the same spirit that united them" (4:94). This scripture of the moral man would be Emerson's new study both in the publications and lectures that would be his new career and in the private journals where he would develop his ideas.

In December 1833, Emerson not only began a new blank book for his journals, but also a new alphabetical system of headings. After some initial quotations the first entry of "Journal A" reads: "This Book is my Savings Bank. I grow richer because I have somewhere to deposit my earnings; and fractions are worth more to me because corresponding fractions are waiting here that shall be made integers by their addition" (4:250–51). This passage provides an especially apt analysis of the nature of Emerson's *Journals*. They usually appear fragmented, but the whole is far greater than the sum of its parts; these fragments take on heightened value when recognized as conveying a complex series of relationships.

Aware of the connections between entries, Emerson often made references within the journal to related passages; and, in this section of the diary, he began to mine them extensively for his lectures and essays. Yet, while his public works offer a tighter development of ideas than do the journals, the journals do have their own special coherence. The complex associations between journal entries, like those between thoughts or memories, are not easily represented by the linear organization of the formal essay. The very fragmentary nature of the diary form, which can make it difficult to recognize the relationships between the scattered ideas, mirrors the complexities of life and thought and induces the reader to recognize the real nature of intellectual processes.

For example, in an early section of "Journal A" Emerson began an entry with a reminiscence about his dead wife: "These last three years are not a chasm—I could almost wish they were—so brilliantly sometimes the vision of Ellen's beauty & love & life come out of the darkness." However, not only do the previous and subsequent entries deal with other, often unrelated matters; but even within the entry Emerson moved his focus from these "sad thoughts" to "the sublime religion" of a Quaker woman of New Bedford (4:263). The orderly treatment of an essay might skip from this reference to Ellen to the next one five months later or move from this discussion of the operation of reminiscence and memory to the next. The diary form leaves the unraveling of its intricate connections to the reader.

Such literary treasure hunts are not for everyone, and Emerson's long and complex diary offers especially difficult ones; however, for those devoted to diary literature these intricacies are likely to be one of its attractions. Emerson, himself a reader of diaries,[9] probably enjoyed this activity. Certainly it fit his belief in the gestalt of beauty he emphasized both in his poem, "Each and All," and on the pages of his diary: "Nothing is beautiful alone. Nothing but is beautiful in the Whole" (5:26).

Even when the reader of Emerson's journals comes upon an entry that has little or no obvious relation to other parts of the work, the passage may still prove of special interest. In 1834 Emerson recounted a story he had heard from an old seaman of "a white whale which was known by the whalemen as Old Tom & who rushed upon the boats which attacked" and of the ship that was "fitted out at New Bedford . . . to take him" (4:265). Emerson's interest in this story, which was one of the sources for Herman Melville's *Moby-Dick,* may have been no more than a freak coincidence, but his record of this incident suggests that these writers shared an interest in the power of nature as an inspiration to heroism. Like Melville, Emerson could admire resourcefulness in the physical world. For example, during his first trip to Europe Emerson praised his ship's captain for qualities Melville must have admired in models for his Ahab: "Here is our stout master worth a thousand philosophers—a man who can strike a porpoise, & make oil out of his blubber, & steak out of his meat . . . who can bleed a sick sailor, and mend the box of his pump" (4:115).

Emerson's journal prompts the reader to make comparisons with other writers of the period. Consider, for example, his comment that going into nature opened his eyes and "let what would pass through them into the soul" so that he ceased caring about his relationship to the physical world and "heeded no more what minute or hour our Massachusetts clocks might indicate" (4:273). Emerson's words almost invite the reader to make a connection with the line in Whitman's "Song of Myself"—"The clock indicates the moment—but what does eternity indicate." It is not necessary to establish a direct line of influence before concluding that the similarity is not just coincidental. Even more obvious and numerous are those passages that show parallels between Emerson and Thoreau.

The journal also helps to show the relationships between Emerson's reading and his thought. Even though he would warn in "The American Scholar" that books were too often an impediment to original thinking, he accepted them as useful for otherwise "idle times." The journal is full of references to, quotations from, and comments on volumes Emerson considered important, including both published diaries and the manuscript diaries of personal acquaintances.

The associations most frequently suggested by passages in the journal are those with Emerson's own published essays. The reader acquainted with those works will find the journal studded with familiar passages. Indeed, many of Emerson's most memorable passages had their origin in the journal. However, while he made important and extensive use of journal material, he does not appear to have used his maturer journals as a place for formal composition. He had used some early journal books to record regular notes for essays or to compose whole drafts, but his published essays make different use of the later journal. While there seems to be a tendency for those journal passages used in the essays to follow the same sequence of ideas in the published work, this pattern is not sufficiently consistent to suggest premeditation. Rather, it seems that the usefulness of the ideas developed in such entries was recognized after the entries were written. It seems likely that the parallel developments of themes in the published works and in the journal may have followed the growth of an idea in Emerson's thoughts. Certainly, the sequence of language and ideas in the essays rarely follows that of the journal for more than a paragraph without significant interruption. It appears that Emerson used his journal to record the idea of the moment and only later found the connection between widely separated entries.

This process fitted well into his conception of the physical universe as a series of seemingly separate elements connected by a vast and complex web of ideal bonds. The journal entries hold the spirit of many of Emerson's most famous lines, but they were rarely borrowed intact. Some alterations were made to polish a rougher, duller, or less precise version in the journal; others were modifications to fit a new context. The following comparison between part of the journal entry for March 2, 1834, and one of the most famous passages in *Nature* indicates both types of alteration have been used:

Journal:
It is very seldom that a man is truly alone. He needs to retire as much from his solitude as he does from society into very loneliness. While I am reading & writing in my chamber, I am not alone though there is nobody there. (4:266–67)

Nature:
To go into solitude, a man needs to retire as much from his chamber as from society. I am not solitary whilst I read and write though nobody is with me. [10]

The version in *Nature* is more concise, more polished in its cadences, but there are other differences between the two. Note that there is a significant change in content. In the journal loneliness was the state sought and solitude the state to be transcended; in *Nature* solitude is the goal. Of course, it may be argued that Emerson's goal did not change, that the meaning of the two versions is the same and only the connotation of words such as *solitude* has been altered. However, one should not overlook the loveliness that Romantics such as Poe attached to *loneliness*. The words *alone* and *solitary* may be synonyms, but *loneliness* and *solitude* are not; few of those declaring a need to be alone would wish to be lonely. A comparison of the two versions suggests that during this period Emerson was moving away from (although not totally abandoning) the melancholy early Romanticism suggested by some of his entries about his dead wife and toward Transcendentalism.

Emerson's use of journal material in his essays presents numerous critical problems. Consider, for example, his modification of the journal entry for April 13, 1834, for the essay, "Self-Reliance":

Journal:
Absolve yourself to the universe, & as God liveth, you shall ray out light & heat,—absolute good. (4:275)

"Self-Reliance":
Absolve yourself to yourself, and you shall have the suffrage of the world.[11]

The sentence structure and some significant phrases are borrowed; but at least on the surface the two messages seem radically different. The journal appears to maintain the existence of an external obligation, the essay to deny it. Even some of the material that follows each of the two versions could be used to support these different readings; the journal emphasizes man's debt to the "immeasurable past," which obligates one to "live for the world," while "Self-Reliance" continues with an argument that one must be prepared to resist the claims of even the most sacred traditions.

Faced with this apparent discrepancy, one might recall that Emerson typically emphasized that seemingly inconsistent points might be joined as part of a higher synthesis. However, a fuller examination shows that the two passages are really compatible. The word *universe* as used in the journal entry refers to things internal as well as external, including "self" and "Creator," while the word *world* in the essay version refers only to the external. These intricate philosophical distinctions and the systems that organized them may not have all been begun in this period of Emerson's life, but a large number of them seem to have flowered then.

The journals show that Emerson had difficulty resolving conflicting elements in his most cherished beliefs. Self-reliance, which he declared to be "the subject that needs most to be presented [and] developed," seemed to jar with his recognition of the "indispensable ministry of friends" (4:269). He would have his "own bosom . . . supply . . . the direction of my course," and follow the "true way" dictated by his own soul; yet he declared that even "the most original writer" could not help but be influenced by "the great writers" who had come before him and "established the conventions of composition" (4:264, 269, 268).

While the creation of material for the published writings that would make Emerson famous is one of the diary's most interesting elements, it was not the only important activity identified in this portion. Here we read of the beginning of his associations with Bronson Alcott and Margaret Fuller and of his second marriage. Emerson's bond to his first wife did not end with this second marriage, but its nature had changed. Six months before marrying Lydia Jackson he wrote in the journal: "I loved Ellen, & love her with an affection that would ask nothing but its indulgence to make me blessed. Yet when she was taken from me, the air was still sweet, the sun was not taken down from my firmament, & however sore was that particular loss, I still felt it was particular, that the Universe remained to us both, that the Universe abode in its light & in its power to replenish the heart with hope" (5:19–20). And even six weeks after his marriage he made the following entry:

Ellen
29 Sept. I am glad of a day when I know what to do in it.[12]
Ellen
Ellen

While these entries reveal a continued attachment to Ellen, Emerson was already choosing "the white future" over "the grey past" (5:187). The achievements he was making and the fame that was soon to come were signs that he was emerging from his "dark night of the soul."

In "Works and Days" Emerson wrote that the physical world is an "illusion" that, hiding "the values of the present time," leads us to reply to the question, "What are you doing?" with "O, nothing." The inspiration for this section of the essay came from a journal entry in which he explored part of the importance of diary keeping. His argument was essentially a secularized version of that used by his Puritan ancestors for their diaries. Failing to recognize some single overwhelming religious experience as evidence of grace, they often turned to their diaries, where they might either recognize such an experience through hindsight or find some pattern of individually insignificant events that would serve as evidence. Emerson came to realize that experiences and ideas that seemed trivial when recorded in the journals might, after a time, "glitter and attract," or reveal a pattern that would yield important truths (7:417–18).

Moreover, Emerson found a special virtue in this "illusion" of nature. He concluded that because our experiences are initially unappreciated, they are allowed to "take their own way & natural shape" and so become beautiful and poetic (7:418). Considering the beauty of such real experience to have significant literary potential, Emerson even went so far as to predict that novels would "give way by & by to diaries or autobiographies."

Emerson's interest in the special qualities of the diary form was further supported by his belief in the supremacy of the individual fact. In 1836 he abandoned a separate notebook journal he had titled "Encyclopedia" (6:115–234). Commenting on this action in his regular journal, Emerson wrote that his goal for that volume had been to record "the net value of all the definitions at which the world had arrived," but that finally he had realized the task was impossible. However, while he discovered that "no diligence can rebuild the Universe in a model by the accumulation or disposition of details," there was another model he could point to and use. Emerson concluded that "the World reproduce[s] itself in miniature in every event that transpires so that all the laws of nature may be read in the smallest fact" (7:302–3). This conclusion can be used to understand his new perception of his own journal. Neither major sections nor the whole could become a model of or for the universe (and, indeed, none of his long and complex essays might so function), but the individual entry as the portrait of the "single fact" might serve. Viewing the journal entry in this way, Emerson's own regard for the diary form was heightened.

Given his endorsement of principles that support the value of diary literature, why didn't Emerson publish his diaries during his lifetime? The answer may be that in his own mind he had published them when he chose "among his experiences" recorded in the journals for his essays (7:418–19). The seeming contradiction may be understood by considering Emerson's view of time. Emerson, or at least the early radically self-reliant spirit who created the optimistic works upon which most of his fame has been based, denied the limitation of time, believing that, "a great man escapes out of the kingdom of time; he puts time under his feet" (5:493). To Emerson, the directional temporal dimension of the diary form was an illusion. Just as widely separated elements of the physical world might have close spiritual ties unperceived by the senses, so temporally separate elements might in "reality" be bound together.

Several pieces of evidence support this view of the relationship of time to Emerson's journalizing. One fact that seems significant is that at many points in his life Emerson kept more than one journal book at a time and so violated the strict chronological sequence. Another is that he frequently reread the diary, a process which often resulted in a new set of temporal connections. Rereading his journal, Emerson not only borrowed from it for lectures and public writings, but also altered its entries. The manuscript is full of deletions and insertions in the original entries as well as comments on or reworked ideas from earlier entries. Still further evidence is Emerson's practice of indexing, which stressed connections between widely separated entries.[13]

The effect of this temporal view for the diary was to enhance its use as a "savings bank" for his public works. Through such use he could surmount the rigidities of time and develop the spiritual connections. A large portion of the diary entries in the journal manuscript for this period are marked over with vertical or diagonal lines, indicating that they had been mined for use in other writings. Of course, the corresponding reduction in entries containing the kind of personal thoughts and activities less easily adapted for public works may be attributable to the increased contentment Emerson felt in both his professional and his domestic life.

This period of Emerson's life and journal was marked by a series of hopeful beginnings. On August 27, 1836, he noted having received "the first proof-sheet of 'Nature.'" And, while he made no mention of its publication two weeks later or of the public reaction to it, it would be the first of a series of publications that would bring the fame that changed his life. In the next months two other significant events occurred. On September 20 he recorded his impressions of the first meeting of what would become the Transcendental Club (5:195), and on October 31 he described his reactions to the birth of his first child: "Last night at 11 o'clock, a son was born to me. Blessed child! a lovely wonder to me, and which makes the universe look friendly to me. How remote from my knowledge, how alien, yet how kind does the Cause of Causes appear! The stimulated curiosity of the father sees graces & instincts which exist, indeed, in every babe, but unnoticed in all the others; the right to see all, know all, to examine nearly distinguishes this relation" (5:234). He would later write that "Hope should be painted with an infant on her arm" (5:257). That Emerson was hopeful about his own future is suggested by his frequent consideration of human greatness throughout this section of the journal.

Perhaps one reason for his strong attraction to his child is that this was one relationship in which he could both feel effectual and break down the physical, emotional, and spiritual barriers that separated him from even his nearest friends. When the newspapers had been persecuting Bronson Alcott, Emerson used his journals to lament his "inefficiency to practical ends," regretting that he could "only comfort my friends by thought, & not by love or by aid" (5:298). In another he wrote: "The most I can be to my fellow man, is the reading of his book, or the hearing of his project in conversation. I approach some . . . with desire & joy. I am led from month to month with an expectation of total embrace & oneness with a noble mind. . . . But man is insular and cannot be touched. Every man is an infinitely repellent orb" (5:328–29). Emerson's attempt to excuse his own difficulties with close personal relationships as a manifestation of a universal problem is not convincing.

Despite strong desires to the contrary, he had difficulty relating to others and could not fully understand their acceptance of him. He frequently used the journal to complain that despite the friendship he was offered he felt isolated: "I have never known a man who had so much good accumulated upon him as I have. Reason, health, wife, child, friends, competence, reputation, the power to inspire, & the power to please. Yet leave me alone a few days, and I creep about as if in expectation of a calamity" (5:45).

There is an essential tension in this part of the diary between Emerson's desire for personal involvement with friends and family, an area in which he was less than successful, and his desire to be a creative artist, an area in which he was very successful. Considering that "literary wealth" was the product of his isolation, he warned himself to "guard . . . [his] moods as anxiously as a miser his money" and even speculated that a writer should not marry or have children (7:420). Yet he could not endure such isolation; he unreservedly praised solitude in

Nature, but in his journal he declared it to be "fearsome & heavy heart-ed" (5:454).

His memories were so tainted that recalling any part of his youth made him "shrink." Even in a reverie about his dead first wife he re-proached himself for the self-doubt that had clouded their relationship:

Ah could I have felt in the presence of [Ellen] . . . as now I feel my own power & hope, & so have offered her in every word & look the heart of a man humble & wise, but resolved to be true & perfect with God, & not as I fear it seemed, the uneasy uncentered joy of one who received in her a good—a lovely good—out of all proportion to his deserts, I might haply have made her days longer & certainly sweeter & at least have recalled her seraph smile without a pang. (5:456)

Here Emerson implies that this new self-reliant "power & hope" had changed him, but this journal entry also suggests that he had not fully achieved this new confidence.

In one entry he recorded a fable of "a simple man" who had grown "so suddenly rich that coming one day into his own stately door & hall" he momentarily forgot it was his and began to fear "encountering the great man who owned it" (5:460). The story may have had an autobiographical application, for there are several journal passages in which Emerson seems to have disbelieved his own growing wealth and reputation. He found it difficult to get used to the fact that he no longer needed to "purse . . . [his] mouth in expectation of any great man," that he was "no man's man," but was free to do what work he wished to do (5:461).

Emerson's influence worked not only through his writings and lec-tures, but also through personal contacts, and his journals document numerous instances in which his values were adopted by his acquain-tances. The nature of such influences was not always obvious or simple, but some seem compelling. Consider, for example, the way the follow-ing excerpt seems to predict the efforts of Thoreau: "If life were long enough among my thousand & one works should be a book of Na-ture. . . . It should contain the Natural history of the woods around my shifting camp for every month in the year. It should tie their as-tronomy, botany, physiology, meteorology, picturesque, & poetry to-gether" (5:25).

Of course, such influences are complex. Writing in another entry that Bronson Alcott would "scorn to exchange" his school for "the presidency of the United States," Emerson called this position "a just example of the true rule of Choice of Pursuit. You may do nothing to get money which is not worth doing on its own account. . . . Nor will the plainly expressed wishes of other people be a reason why you should do to oblige them what violates your sense" (5:419). This "true rule" Emerson articulated follows the same basic concept Thoreau would use in "Life without Principle," and is similar to ideas presented in *Walden.*[14]

The journal also provides evidence of the influence of others on Emerson. We find this influence in Emerson's comments on his reading, correspondence, and personal contacts. In one entry he wrote about a dispute he had had with Thoreau when the two were walking to Walden. Arguing about the propriety of the private ownership of "God's Earth,"[15] Emerson suggested that Thoreau make a poem about his belief. However, when Thoreau replied that a poem "ought to sing itself," and that such conscious manipulation of an abstract principle was "no longer the Idea itself," it was Emerson who was influenced to write, eventually expanding on his journal account of Thoreau's response as the basis for one of his own lectures (7:143–44).

No event recorded in the journal had a greater influence on Emerson than did the death of his son. On January 28, 1842, he wrote in his diary, "Yesterday night at 15 minutes after eight my little Waldo ended his life" (7:163). As with the death of his first wife almost eleven years earlier, this tragedy radically affected his life and his diary. Indeed, in some ways Waldo's death was more disturbing than Ellen's had been because it undermined the elaborate philosophical system that Emerson had used to reconcile him to his previous loss. His early, almost unreservedly optimistic, Transcendentalism seemed inadequate, and no easy response was possible. In the journal he had used the line, "you plant a tree for your son," to express his belief that the motive for creativity was in its service to future generations; but now his son was dead.

Emerson had once declared that his life, that all life, was "a May game" (7:208), but four months after Waldo's death he wrote, "If I should write an honest diary what should I say? Alas that life has halfness, shallowness. I have almost completed thirty nine years and have not yet adjusted my reaction to my fellows on the planet, or to my own work. Always too young or too old, I do not satisfy myself; how can I satisfy others?" (7:458). Even two years after the tragedy he admitted not only that had he been unable to deal with his grief, but also that this experience in the physical world had made it difficult for him to deal with the spiritual one on which his system depended: "I had no experience nor progress to reconcile me to the calamity whose anniversary returned the second time last Saturday. . . . The astonishment of life is the absence of any reconciliation between the theory & practice of life. Our sanity, our genius, the prized reality, the law is apprehended now & then for a serene & profound moment . . . is then lost for months or years, & found again for an interval to be lost again" (9:65). Emerson, who had rejected spiritual and creative impotence as a lame excuse, labeling "discontent" as "want of self-reliance" and "infirmity of will,"[16] now confided to his journal: "Sorrow makes us all children again destroys all differences of intellect. The wisest know nothing" (8:165).

Some journal passages written after Waldo's death echo entries Emerson had written while his son was alive. The transmutation of the same perceptions from humor to melancholy offers a remarkable opportunity to observe the effects of grief. In early entries Emerson declared that two apples which "the dear little Angel has gnawed. . . . are worth a barrel of apples that he has not touched," and he found joy in the boy's childish behavior and pronunciation: "Little Waldo cheers the whole house with his moving calls to the cat, to the birds, to the flies, 'Pussy cat come see Waddo! Liddel Birdy come see Waddo! Pies! Pies! come see Waddo'" (7:42–43).

After Waldo's death Emerson, in striking violation of some of his most cherished principles, converted these exaltations of present delight into sad idols of the past:

What he looked upon is better, what he looked not upon is insignificant. How much more all the particulars of the daily economy for he had touched with his lively curiosity every trivial fact & circumstance in my household the hard coal & the soft coal which I put into my stove; the wood of which he brought his little quota for grandmother's fire, the hammer, the pincers & file he was so eager to use; the microscope, the magnet, the little globe & every trinket & instrument in the study; the loads of gravel on the meadow the nests in the henhouse. . . . For every thing he had his own name & way of thinking, his own pronunciation & manner and every word came mended from that tongue. A boy of early wisdom, of a grave & even majestic deportment, of a perfect gentleness. (8:163–64)

In these reminiscences Emerson transmuted all that Waldo had done or said into poetry. Recalling Waldo's request to keep at the side of his bed a bell that he had been making, Emerson wrote the speech in language too elevated and cadences too rhythmical to have been like those of the original:

But Mamma I am afraid that it will alarm you. It may sound in the middle of the night and it will be heard over the whole town, it will be louder than ten thousand hawks and it will be heard across the water, and in all the countries. It will be heard all over the world.
It will sound like some great glass thing which falls down and breaks to pieces. (8:166)

One sentence after this excerpt Emerson ripped two pages out of the diary. Perhaps the grief they contained was too great to keep, perhaps they were used for "Threnody," his elegy for his son.

"Threnody" is an effective poem, but the journal suggests that its argument for the child's immortality—"What is excellent, / As God lives, is permanent"—was less than effective in providing solace to the mourning father. Emerson did find an answer, but it required an alteration of his philosophy. The most obvious change was a movement away from the confident, radical Transcendentalism of his earlier period to a new and moderate skepticism. In his essay "The Transcendentalist" Emerson argued the superiority of idealism over materialism by comparing the physical and spiritual sides of reality to opposite sides of a tapestry. According to this image, both spirit and matter are real and part of the same whole, but following the analogy of the tapestry, the ideal is primary and the material subordinate. In "Montaigne, the Skeptic," written after the death of Waldo, Emerson argued that both the idealist and the materialist claimed too much for their positions. Here, he portrayed spirit and matter as two sides of a coin; this image gives neither side supremacy.

The course of Emerson's journal followed this same subtle change in position. The subject matter became more concrete and the value given to the physical world was slightly but evidently increased. This new Emerson of "Montaigne" argued that while individuals might lean to either the spiritual or the physical side of nature, the ideal to be sought was some balanced character. But Emerson found himself unable to achieve this goal. Still complaining about his inability to act in the physical world, Emerson declared that his "capital defect" was "the want of animal spirits." The concrete achievements of others made him feel cowardly, his "fear" making such achievements, "as much out of my possibility as the prowess of Coeur de Lion" (9:18). This situation became even more intolerable when he felt that he was losing his audience because those who read his books and attended his lectures expected him to go beyond abstract philosophy and become an active reformer (9:49). The journal contains some entries in which Emerson did attempt some practical actions, such as his endorsement of a controversial antislavery lecture, but he never became truly active in the manner of Alcott and Thoreau.

Emerson's later diaries seem increasingly concerned with the physical world, such as the events of the Civil War; still, the journals show that he never abandoned his fundamental concern for the spiritual. Struggle and death, his own aging and that of his friends seem always balanced by the sympathy of nature and imagination. In an entry written late in his life Emerson recalled his childhood, when the most casual experiences were cause for amazement:

When a boy I used to go to the warves, & pick up shells out of the sand which vessels had brought as ballast, & also plenty of stones, gypsum, which I discovered would be luminous when I rubbed two bits together in a dark closet, to my great wonder—& I do not know why luminous, to this day . . . and the charm of drawing vases by scrawling with ink in heavy random lines & then doubling the paper so as to make another side symmetrical—what was chaos becoming symmetrical. . . .

Still earlier, what silent wonder is waked in the boy by blowing bubbles from soap & water with a pipe. (16:263)

Emerson's sense of wonder never left him.

Amos Bronson Alcott (1799–1888)

The most highly praised of the American Transcendentalists praised Bronson Alcott. In his own journal Emerson described Alcott as "the most extraordinary man and the highest genius of the time. He is a Man. He is erect. He sees: let who ever be overthrown. . . . Life he would have & enact & not nestle into any cast off shell & form of old time. . . . Wonderful is his vision. The steadiness and scope of his eye rebukes all before it and we little men creep about ashamed" (5:328). Thoreau immortalized Bronson Alcott on the pages of *Walden*. Expanding his journal entry for May 9, 1853, he called Alcott, "the man of the most faith of any alive. . . . A true friend of man; almost the only friend of human progress . . . [and] perhaps the sanest man . . . of any I chance to know." Thoreau went on to predict that "though comparatively disregarded now, when his day comes, laws unsuspected will take effect and masters of families will come to him for advice."[17] But that day never came. He continues to attract some interest, but too often his only fame seems to be as the father of Louisa May Alcott.[18]

Thoreau too had been neglected during his lifetime, but he attained posthumous fame through his works. Those works that Alcott wrote for publication never attracted great attention.[19] The greatness Emerson and Thoreau praised lay elsewhere. A passage in Emerson's journal preserves Alcott's perceptions of his own significance. Alcott claimed that while "every man . . . is a revelation and ought to write his record . . . few [should do so] with the pen." He believed that the "book" in which he would write "all his thoughts" would be an experimental school he kept. Following the Emersonian model, however, Alcott's "book" would be not an institution, but the actions with which it was created and sustained; "autobiography," Alcott insisted, "is the best book."[20]

Fortunately, an approximation of this "book" exists in the surviving portions of the detailed diary Alcott kept for over seventy years. Made up of over sixty surviving volumes containing nearly five million words, his journals are equal in length to the combined journals of Emerson and Thoreau. Unfortunately, the expense and time required for a complete edition has prevented the full publication of them. However, Odell Shepard's two-volume abridgment is widely available; some long continuous sections of the journal have been published; and more, surely, will be published in the future.[21]

Even the huge diary that survives is not complete. Alcott began his first journal when he was only twelve, but those volumes written prior to 1826 were burned in 1833. Odell Shepard suggested that Alcott may have destroyed the volumes himself since his values had undergone a change, and he might have felt that they "dealt too much with external facts and too little with ideas."[22] Six more volumes were lost or destroyed, and so there are only fifty of the annual volumes for the years 1826–82.

Despite the loss of the earliest journals, we know why Alcott began his diary and how the record developed. In later entries he revealed that in his youth he had accidentally found his mother's journal "hidden away in an old oaken chest." That discovery, he explained, "set me out in this chase after myself, and continued it till fixed by habit . . .

[it became] a natural part of the days—like the rising and setting sun"
(5/9/69). In another manuscript volume Alcott wrote an autobiographical account that gives some idea of his intentions and early practice.
Under the date 1812 he explained: "I began keeping a diary of my
doings with some entrances of the weather and events . . . [including
some] of my readings and a catalogue of the books read with a list of
my own little library."[23] The implication of this statement is that the
early diary started as a record of external events. Alcott later expanded
the diary so that it could serve as a repository of ideas as well as events:

I look back upon these pages whereon I have imagined some dim and imperfect signs of my spiritual and intellectual life—some emblematic hints of what
I have been doing and designing—some notes that indicate, where in the
realm of space and time, I lived and felt and thought and acted. As I read the
written words the past comes up before me and I commune with my past-
self—my former states of thought—I trace the history of ideas from their
embryon forms to their maturer shapings.[24]

The record also served Alcott as "a psychological Diary" containing
his "inmost doings and endeavorings." He wrote that "no important
thought, emotion or purpose has transpired within me that has not
been noted therein. . . . I have unveiled myself without the least attempt at concealment—This book has been my confessional" (6/28/
39). Alcott made such "confessions" openly, showing his diary to many
of his circle, including Emerson, Thoreau, and Fuller. He also showed
his journal to his wife, who occasionally complained about some of the
content, especially when it referred to her. Even though Alcott pro-
tested that he had only written from his "convictions and what seemed
. . . plain fact," she placed some of these passages "under the ban of
her scissors," removing them from the manuscript (2/2/39).

Alcott was acutely aware of the complex nature of the diary. When
he began to make an alphabetical index of it, he found the task extremely difficult because the topics were so "various, and innumerable
relations are implied, yet not stated." He complained that he found
"little objectivity" and that too much had been "left in vagueness" (6/
28/39). However, even though the diary expanded beyond its original
limits to include philosophical speculations, it remained true to its
origins. Unlike the journals of Emerson and Thoreau, Alcott's personal
record preserves the shaping form of external events and is more worthy
to be classed as a variation of the diary proper than as a journal of

internal musings. (Alcott himself used both the words *diary* and *journal* in referring to his work.)

Alcott's diary as it developed had many uses; it is too large and too varied for any simple definition of purpose. For example, in addition to sixty-one volumes of the regular diary, he wrote at least five travel diaries entitled "Itineraries," four volumes of regular dated entries devoted to observations of the development of his children, as well as other notebooks related to the diaries.

In one relatively early journal entry Alcott reconstructed events from his earlier life. One of the favorite books of his youth was Bunyan's *Pilgrim's Progress,* and in this biographical section he portrayed himself as being on a kind of heroic pilgrimage to a region beyond the evils and limitations of the material world. Alcott deserves credit for achieving as much as he did without the educational advantages of most of the others in his circle, but his autobiographical account seems too egotistical in its praise of his own desire for knowledge and too negative in its attitude toward everyone else and to nature itself to win a reader's unqualified admiration:

In childhood confined to the narrow range of thought,—which the observation of the few objects and incidents in a small isolated town could furnish— thrown into the society of ignorance and selfishness, and removed from the means of moral & intellectual improvement. A mind ardent in the pursuit of knowledge, and a heart seeking for happiness in the sterile soil of my native town, and its cold frozen climate, without books—without friends to which I could apply for instruction and happiness—an independent spirit sensible of its degradation and lacking the means of which in its happiness. (12/4/29)

Alcott went on to tell how by the age of fifteen he was "planning schemes for future employment and acquisition and moralizing on vices and follies of . . . [his fellow] townsmen," but he tells the reader nothing about the nature of these "follies" or how he escaped such errors. Far from having a positive impact, such an assertion of moral superiority is likely to make a reader skeptical about subsequent claims. For example, when Alcott went on to write that he usually differed with his father on "points of thought and action," but nevertheless remained "submissive and obedient" to his parent's wishes, he seems to be betraying a hidden resentment. Describing himself as "the pride of my mother, her favorite—the *servant* of my younger brother, the object of ridicule among the forward and impetuous of my companions," Alcott revealed still more of the pain of his adolescence, probably more than he was aware of himself (12/4/29). Such lack of insight into his own limitations primed him for failure.

Alcott's first major failure came only a few years later. Although he had already declared that, as a youth he had been sufficiently aware of "follies and vices" to ridicule them in others, he soon wrote that when he was eighteen he was "unacquainted with the world, its follies and vices." Alcott claimed that his failure in business was the result of his "open, sincere" nature. But, while admitting that he neglected his business "for intellectual pleasures," Alcott still insisted that he had gone into debt, "through confidence in [society's] integrity," and that he became "the recipient of disgrace for having been honest and confiding" (12/4/28). Such contradictions and self-serving claims further cast doubt on the accuracy of Alcott's self-portrait.

Throughout his life Alcott would view himself as superior to most of the world. In one entry he wrote a list of those living men he considered "the freemen and the brave, by whom great principles are to be honored amongst us." These he divided into two groups, including his own name with those of Emerson, Ripley, Dwight, and Parker, in the higher, "more effective" class, and placing those of Channing, Dewey, and Garrison in the lower class (10/Week 42/38). Alcott could only maintain this positive self-image by rejecting the world's standards. Perhaps his string of "failures" in those areas that the world might view as signs of success may be attributable to a need to discredit such standards. The journal treats several incidents in which Alcott, on the verge of success, would take some action that would "salvage" defeat.

Returning home at age twenty-three, Alcott was heavily in debt and severely ill. He gradually regained his health and attempted to regain his reputation by teaching school in Connecticut. It was during this period that he wrote the first of the surviving volumes of his diary. This volume, titled "No 1 School Journal—Remarks and Reflections During the Summer Term of the Cheshire Pestalozzian School," was focused on his teaching. Alcott was drawn to teaching as a means to influence others, and one of the functions of this diary was as a place to examine the effect of that influence. However, while his educational innovations drew favorable comments outside the communities in which he taught, they repeatedly aroused opposition within, forcing him to leave and seek new employment.

Just as Whitman would claim to have been falsely accused of "seeking to destroy institutions," so Alcott recognized that his attempts at educational innovation would make him the target of similar charges:

"Those who in modern times attempt in education anything different from the old established modes, are by many regarded as publick innovators on the peace and order of society, as persons desirous of destroying the structure which secures present happiness, and of substituting in its place anarchy & confusion. They are regarded by some as dangerous, and by others as ignorant, and imbecile members of society" (9/22/26). Alcott firmly believed that God did not reveal truth to a people as a group, "but to a *Gifted Spirit* among them" (1/2/35), and despite public rejection of his ideas, he believed himself a prophet of that truth.

Alcott set himself lofty goals. He wished to devote his life to the establishment of "the reign of truth and reason—and [to] arrange the laws of society—our systems of education— in accordance with the laws of nature." He wrote, "We are not mistaken— our theory is based on the nature of man—and the designs and purposes of his existence" (6/14/28). This last excerpt offers only one example of Alcott's use, in early volumes of the journal, of an editorial or royal *we* in place of *I,* a practice that suggests his belief in his mission to speak as an authority in advising the world. This usage also appears in the entry in which he confided his intention to propose to Abigail May: "We are unwilling that she should engage in this school with the hope of continuing in it when we leave—for we are very desirous—and are becoming every day more interested in her—that she should assist in the more desirable situation which we propose for ourselves in a school of an higher order" (6/1/28).

On May 23, 1830, Bronson married Abigail, and in March of the next year Anna, their first daughter, was born. Alcott was delighted to hear that he "was indeed a father" (3/16/31). Obviously enjoying the role, he declared that he was happier than he had been "at any former period" because of an increased "faith that reposes on Providence" and a new love that bound him more securely to "human nature." However, when he declared "Childhood hath saved me," he was referring to more than the usual joys of parenthood. His children were "objects of great delight," and "the charm of . . . [his] domestic life," but they also bolstered his confidence in his principles. They served him as "living manifestations of the theories of my intellect . . . [and] models of our common nature from whence these *theories* are in no small degree framed" (1/21/35).

Three months after Anna's birth Alcott's simple joy of parenthood yielded to a more serious conception, the creation of a special kind of diary, "the history of one human mind commenced in infancy and faithfully narrated by the parent until the child should be able to assume the work himself, and carried onward all the vicissitudes of life to its close." Such a work, Alcott believed, "would be a treasure of inconceivably more value to the world than all the systems which philosophers have built concerning the mind up to this day. It would be a history of human nature to this day."[25] Titling his volume *History of an Infant,* Alcott began with the first cries at birth and followed not only with an account of the child's physical maturation but also with her psychological development. He was an early advocate of psychology as a science, insisting that, "Human nature must be studied as other sciences" (1/23/32).

The nature of this project suggests that Alcott believed that one single case study with sufficient detail would be better than more generalized but less detailed systems, that a single life might symbolize all. Although most modern experimental psychologists would hardly consider the generalization from a single uncontrolled observation to be scientific, Alcott's procedures are not too different from Jean Piaget's attempts to learn about human development by observing his own children. Expecting that such a record would be publishable, Alcott soon amassed a sizable volume, and he later repeated the process with his other children. In each case he hoped that his record would lead the child to the creation of her own diary, and in several cases this hope was realized.

Alcott kept detailed records of each new behavior or tendency in the developing characters of his children, but he was not content to be only a passive observer. Both his regular diary and the special volumes of observations on his children show his attempts to manipulate his daughters' characters, rewarding and punishing according to his conceptions of right and wrong. The diaries suggest that, at least in their early lives, Alcott's second daughter, Louisa, received more punishment than did his eldest daughter, Anna. Anna, whom Alcott considered a creature of the "imagination," had a character that, like his own, favored the "ideal" and showed "only a minor inclination and a limited ability to affect" her wishes. Louisa, on the other hand, seemed to him a creature of the "understanding," favoring the practical and able to attain her goals "by force of will" (11/5/34). Since she differed from his model, he determined to alter her nature.

Alcott took the experiences he recorded in his diaries of his own children and applied the principles he derived from them to his teaching. His use of the diaries seems to have been beneficial in that his school did begin to prosper. The period from 1833 to 1836 was an important one in Alcott's intellectual development. In 1833 the journals trace his exposure to the writings of Plato and Coleridge that shaped his early Transcendentalism.[26] The following year he discovered the German literature he declared more supportive of his views than that of the English writers with whom he had been most familiar: "How have I been vainly seeking to feed myself on husks!" (4/22/34) He came to feel that he was "still much wallowed in the *actual,*" and needed to devote himself to the spiritual reality, to the idea "purified of all its fancies, and made free from all that bewilders and dazzles" (2/8/35).

In 1834 Alcott left Philadelphia and opened the Temple School in Boston; and, as it began to prosper, he became active in social causes (6/14/36). For example, his journals for 1835 have several entries referring to his involvement in the antislavery movement. During this period he began his friendship with Emerson, and on September 19, 1836, he joined Emerson in founding the Transcendental Club.

Long before Emerson would popularize a self-reliant rejection of the ideas that majority view was automatically correct and that the printed word deserved unquestioning veneration, Alcott had reached some of the same conclusions: "The number and age of those who advocate any particular doctrine is no test of its truth, but, on the contrary, is an indication of its incorrectness" (6/7/27). He found that though books might be useful in dealing with "doubts and uncertainties," they were "imperfect"; therefore, their tendency to "awe many into implicit belief" made them a threat to both self-reliance and a social progress. Alcott's answer was to rebel, to "dare to be singular." Drawn to action, he wanted all men to act at once rather than spend their time debating what to do (12/6/26).

While Thoreau is justly famous for his "Civil Disobedience," not all of the ideas or actions he described in it were original with him. Some were adapted from or modeled after those of Alcott. Long before Thoreau went to prison for nonpayment of his taxes, Alcott had risked the same fate; however, his taxes were paid for him before he could be jailed. Like Thoreau, Alcott concluded that the truly self-reliant man did not need the state to protect his rights and would be better off without it: "The state is man's pantry, at best, and filled at an immense cost. . . . Let it go. Heroes will live on Nuts, and freemen house themselves under the clefts of the rocks sooner than sell their liberty for the pottage of slavery" (2/undated/47).

Alcott was, indeed, more involved in such causes than most of his friends. Emerson in his own diary had complained of being unable to be active. After spending a week as Emerson's guest, Alcott declared in his own journal that the experience taught him what he was: "I apprehend my genius the more clearly . . . by comparison with his." Alcott concluded that, unlike Emerson, he was not a scholar: "My might is not in my pen. . . . My organ is action and voice rather. I am an actor and a sayer rather than a writer. I do not detach my thoughts from my life." Alcott tried to console himself with the notion that his was the better role: "I act rather than observe; insee and foresee, rather than live in memory." Such traits, he believed, made him superior to scholars. "I am rather a study for scholars. I will let them analyze and write" (5/13/39).

But Alcott found his ability to act was also limited. He could not even communicate in ordinary society: "To most my speech is unintelligible and hath terms that have small currency in the markets and shops of the actual!" (1/Week 2/38). Unable to handle the routine affairs of the material world, he declared them to be beneath him. When a butcher took advantage of him, he criticized neither the butcher's deceit nor his own ineptitude, but rather attacked a world that necessitated such mundane activities: "What have I to do with butchers? Am I to go smelling about markets? Both are an offense to me" (2/5/39).

After repeatedly failing to earn enough to reduce his huge debts or, at times, even to support his family, Alcott tried to rationalize, "Man can live on his own faith if his faith be fastened on Love and Wisdom. 'Tis not necessary that *external goods* should enter into the supply. Wiser is he who, in the absence of these, retreats into his own spirit, and . . . lives out the delights of the inner life—triumphing over space and time, by the activity of his own thought" (4/28/34). Alcott did have his doubts about the consequences of his neglect of the physical world. In one entry he confessed, "I have so long lived an inward reflective life that the relations of external things to my temporal prosperity have been almost lost sight of. . . . I cling too closely to the *ideal* to take the necessary advantage of the practical . . . and my wife and children, suffer from this neglect" (4/27/34). However, when his devoted wife distrusted his judgment, Alcott dismissed her doubts. In response to her complaint that she could not see "whence shall come the bread for herself and little ones," he answered, "Neither do I see with eyes of sense; but I know that a purpose like mine must yield bread for the hungry and clothe the naked, and I wait not for the arithmetic of this matter" (4/23/39).

In the "Mast-head" chapter of *Moby-Dick* Melville criticized those "pantheists" who, climbing up to the crow's-nest, might be lulled by the beauty of nature and their own optimistic view of the universe until their very existence was in jeopardy. Alcott by his own admission was a suitable example of such an individual: "How apt am I to ascend and lose sight of things of sense, to climb the ladder to the topmost round, and there reel with the giddy prospect stretching off into indistinctness and bewilderment. Am I caught in the net of a wildly-roving fancy? . . . Verily, an Ideal glitters in my spirit" (10/18/34).

Alcott could be critical of some aspects of his performance. He repeatedly acknowledged his limitations as a writer and even labeled this deficiency as one of the primary causes for his failure to gain popular recognition and the financial security it could bring:

My ideas are better than my style, and for many ideas, distinct and vivid in my own mind, I have no sign, This more than any thing else, is, I believe, the cause of my failure and of the complaint not infrequently made that I am *mystical*. My ideas are, I believe, clear . . . The obscurity lies in the language which I employ. . . . I need terms expressive of innate selections of the details of the subject to bring my conceptions down from their generalizing in the intellect. (4/22/34)

In another entry Alcott criticized his style as lacking those details and "destitute of [that] wit & humor" that might enliven it; he had not, he complained, taken the time to practice the "ease, grace, clearness [and] strength" that his ideas demanded (4/8/30, 8/4/35).

Yet Alcott himself realized that his style was not the only obstacle to his attainment of popular recognition, but he declared that he was content to be "too abstract, too general in . . . application and too metaphysical in . . . character" (4/8/30). Reading Alcott's diary of this period, Emerson offered a more positive evaluation. Although his praise was not without qualification, his comments reflect Alcott's own assessment that his failures were only the incomplete realization of a high purpose; however, Emerson offered no more than a hope that Alcott's purpose might be realized:

I have read with interest Mr. Alcott's journal in MS for 1835. He has attained at least to a perfectly simple and elegant utterance. There is no inflation & no cramp in his writing. I complained that there did not seem to be quite that facility of association which we expect in the man of genius & which is to marry his work with all nature. . . . [But] whatever defects as fine writers such men have it is because colossal foundations are not for summerhouses but for temples and cities. (6:170)

Such comments held no practical suggestion about how Alcott might better communicate his ideas to the public, and Alcott could only console himself with the hope, "Time will make me *intelligible*"; but too often he despaired that his most attentive audience was composed of the plants in his garden, "the attentive Nature in which I abide and toil" (8/4/35, 7/4/46).

Sometimes Alcott's words and ideas were generally "intelligible," but in those cases the response could prove disastrous. In 1836, two years before Emerson's popularity would be significantly threatened by the harsh reaction to his "Address" to the Divinity School, Alcott published similar and even more unpopular views. His *Conversations with Children on the Gospels* not only hurt his popular reputation, but threatened the school on which his livelihood depended.

Alcott's *Conversations* consisted, to a great extent, of transcriptions of Socratic dialogues he held with his students. Starting these discussions from scriptural passages, he led his students to affirm the divinity within all men. In affirming this principle common in American Transcendentalism, Alcott made statements that were interpreted as arguing against the divinity of Jesus. The following passage from the diary of that period expresses sentiments similar to those in his *Conversations:*

Man is God conditioned—God subdivided from himself in order to look backward upon himself. He that doth not believe himself a God, hath lost all sense, all remembrance of his father. . . .
The man shall be stoned, even now, that shall utter what Jesus of Nazareth uttered two milleniums ago . . . that "I and my father are one." (1/Week 4/ 37)

Reviewers attacked Alcott's book and the man himself, condemning him for diving too deeply into "solemn mysteries" (Insert 3/Week 13/ 37).

The disastrous effects of the *Conversations* were not immediately apparent. In an entry written early in 1837 Alcott proclaimed that he had "A sure authentic instinct . . . of the *Idea* that I am striving to incorporate to the sense of my race; it is this that quickens my faith amidst all hindrance. . . . I anticipate the approval of the coming age: the fame, eternal truth that now announces its law, through my special will, shall in due time find its injunctions through other, and all men" (1/Week 1/37).

It was at this time and in this spirit of confidence that Alcott chose to alter the nature of his diary. He was not dissatistifed with his record; indeed, he found it "both interesting and useful—serving to fix the fluid, and otherwise evanescent elements of life, and give them a moment's reality and permanence in consciousness . . . [preserving] whatever there may be for future value and use, so that nothing of life shall be . . . lost." However, he decided that it was more important that he should "seemingly forget chronologies and annals and dwell on the . . . pedigrees of things; seeing these in eternal relations." He would still preserve "historical sequence," but would record his material in weekly units, "omitting to state special days unless by way of illustration." In this way he hoped to devalue the importance of time and show it to be "but the web in which spirit weaves its events [which] . . . colour the fabrick" (1/Week 1/37).

In closing his diary for the year 1836 Alcott wrote "I enter upon a new year with hopes of accomplishing more during its course than I have heretofore" (12/31/36). But 1837 proved a year of trial. Enrollment at his school decreased until he was forced to close it; and, falling into ill health, he even allowed his diary to lapse. After his recovery he opened a new school, but found himself "doomed" to "Quiddle, quiddle, on half a dozen souls" (10/Week 39/37). Even Dr. Channing, who had long been a friend and guide in spiritual matters, deserted him. On his thirty-eighth birthday he complained in the diary: "One half my days are gone, almost and small time remains to complete my work, whatever it shall be. For of this not yet have I a clear vision. Yet now . . . my hand is without service. I wait with due patience . . . as this year has deprived me of the opportunity of worthy labor in the actual, perchance the next shall restore my might" (11/Week 47/37). On the last day of 1837 Alcott called upon his soul to "Awake! . . . Enter into the new year that even now is dawning into the light of thy senses . . . put on the perfect, become the ideal" (12/31/37). But, although he used his diary to try to convince himself that the difficulties he had experienced were "precious" in providing "discipline," throwing him on his "own resources," sharpening his "faculties . . .

for work," and teaching him "self insight" and "the dignity of standing alone" (11/Week 47/37), he also betrayed his despair in several entries, such as the following:

> No man lives more [a] recluse than I. Seldom do I spend an hour with a friend. Not often do I read a book. I am self-subsistent, yet not from choice. How do I sigh for society! How do I yearn for sympathy! and have neither. I suppose there is no possibility of such delights at present. My studies lead me aside from the thoroughfares of ordinary thought. My sympathies cluster around the ideal and withdraw me from the actual wherein most hearts beat. . . . Thus I am sundered from the society and sympathy of my kind, and am an exile, dwelling in the distant yet fairy lands of thought; and therein do I find but now and then a brother exile to whom I can unbosom my soul, without profanation, and in simple faith. . . . I am a stranger on the earth and speak an unknown tongue. The fairy island wherein I have my heart is an unknown planet! It appears not on the charts. (1/Week 2/38)

In the next year Alcott found himself unable to sustain adequate enrollment in his school, and by the spring of 1839 he concluded: "I earn little or nothing in this miserable school; nor am I laboring toward any prospective good in it. There is no school in the land on which I can practice my art. I am not of the time, nor place, nor custom . . . and must work on my own purpose amidst every obstacle" (4/23/39). Finding his labors unappreciated, Alcott used his diary to confirm his decision to abandon teaching.

This period also brought personal tragedy. The Alcotts already had three daughters, but two of Mrs. Alcott's pregnancies had ended with miscarriages and another in a stillbirth. Alcott was determined to have a son and planned to name the child "Hoper" to represent his own overriding hope in the face of discouragements.[27] Unfortunately, the boy born on April 6, 1839, died shortly after birth. The five leaves of the diary for that date have been either cut or torn out, an action that prompts comparison with Emerson's after the death of his son Waldo; but some of Alcott's sorrow is preserved in the diary entry for the next day: "This morning at nine o'clock I saw this bud of a son, nipt ere it had bloomed, fade into the ground. He was laid in the tomb of his ancestry and reposes beside the other of the dead. I return to the living and would minister to their growth" (4/7/39).

Though a time of great difficulty for Alcott, 1839 was a year of great importance for his diary keeping. He was certainly exceptionally prolific during this period, writing over nine hundred pages of manuscript in six months and asserting that he was "better pleased" with it than with his previous volumes (6/28/39). However, Alcott seems to have been still unconvinced that he had found the proper form for his journal, for in the next year's volume he radically altered it. The entries became more condensed and epigrammatic, a change that one biographer suggests may have been an attempt to "imitate Emerson's style of journalizing."[28] Alcott had regularly written entries several pages long, but the last entries for the volume of 1840 are only a few lines.

The year 1839 also marked a turning point in Alcott's career, for when he closed his school, he also decided that his new mission must be "to parents." He concluded that only after they were converted would he be allowed to teach their children. He proposed "to enter at once upon this ministry" (6/22/39). This idea was not new to Alcott, who had long felt that he had a special "mission on earth." He had previously written in his diary that he wished to expand his audience, to write a "*Life of the Human Spirit . . .* not as it reveals itself in *childhood* pure and untried, but as it discloses itself amid the temptations and trials of terrestrial existence" (3/8/35).

Except for the diary of a trip to England from May to October 1842, Alcott's journals for 1841 through 1843 were lost or destroyed in Albany in August 1844.[29] Those for 1844 and 1845 are also missing. There is some reason to suspect that the loss of the diaries for these periods may not have been totally accidental. Alcott's destruction of his earliest volumes raises some cause for suspicion. So does his own entry early in the first volume after the missing ones: "All that I have written is quite worthy of the flames. What with the loss of my papers at Albany and these I have burned today, I feel somewhat relieved. When nature is not unseemly, why mar and distort her countenance? Art is then art only when it beautifies and ennobles its objects." Alcott then went on to regret the loss of one manuscript and some letters he had received, but does not even mention his diaries.[30] At least as telling a piece of evidence is the form of the diaries that follow the break. They are significantly different in nature and appearance from the earlier ones. Those of the late 1830s are written in a neat hand on large white pages. The diaries for the late 1840s are hastily and sloppily scrawled in small blue-paged copybooks. His entries are no longer full and regular. They are even briefer than those in the 1840 volume and, at times, are only sketchy notes. The first half of the 1840s including the period of the lost journals seems almost to have divided Alcott's record into two separate diaries.

A good deal of what is known about Alcott's life during the years of the lost diaries comes from his wife's diary for 1841–42, entitled "Diary at Cottage Concord." In a note inserted over forty years later Abigail Alcott wrote, "I value this journal of 1841–42 more than any subsequent one, because it was a period in my life more full of hardships, doubts, fears, adversities; struggles for my children, efforts to maintain cheerfulness and good discipline, under poverty and debt— misapprehension and disgrace." Several pages have been torn out of the manuscript and the first extant entry is for October 8, 1841, Mrs. Alcott's forty-first birthday. Three months later Bronson Alcott was "preparing for his voyage across the Atlantic." Mrs. Alcott dreaded this separation. On a page overwritten with the words "patient endurance" she wrote: "But to seek to serve mankind should he engage on the other side of the Atlantic?" and accused her husband of "robbing my dear children of their birthrights." However, she not only knew that her husband required "this change of all things" and "the presence of his transatlantic friends," but also hoped that the change might ease strains on their marriage.

The journal of Alcott's travel to England is of some interest. He was pleased by the praise he received by English followers but pained by the "din and huddle" of London. He found its "magnificent" architecture designed for the "comfort and use" of the body rather than the soul, each of its inhabitants an antagonistic "fortification," without "repose, tenderness [or] poise" (6/6–7/42). Even Carlyle seemed "somber" and "pitiless," devoted to working with the dead past instead of "living humanity" (6/25–7/5/42). However, in England he found admirers who strengthened his conviction in his own purpose.

Earlier, Alcott had scorned Emerson's suggestion that he abandon his school in order to travel in Europe. Indeed, Emerson recorded in his journal, "Alcott holds his school in so high regard that he would scorn to exchange it for the presidency of the United States. The school is his Europe" (5:419). Now, England seemed the only place he could find an admiring audience.

Among his English admirers was Charles Lane, who followed his idol to America and purchased a farm in Harvard, Massachusetts, which was to be used as the site for a utopian community. The farm, renamed Fruitlands, proved an impractical proposition. In his diary for 1848 Alcott, after quoting Carlyle's criticism that the project was "an air-castle . . . that looks well at a distance, but will secure no one from real wet and wind," added that it still served as "a measuring of his thought with the men and institutions of his time" (4/2/48).

The period after the failure of Fruitlands was a trying time for Alcott and certainly must have provided the material for a dramatic diary, but we must rely on the descriptions of others to hint about what might be in these lost volumes. Emerson described the Alcott of this period as a "magnificent dreamer brooding as ever on the renewal or re-edification of the social fabric after ideal law, heedless that he has been uniformly rejected by every class to whom he has addressed himself." For Emerson, Alcott's situation was particularly "pathetic" because, this "wandering emperor, from year to year making his rounds of visits from house to house of such as do not exclude him," imagined himself "the only realist" (9:50).

It may be more than coincidence that the resumption of the diary in 1846 seems to have coincided with a return of Alcott's life to a calmer, more settled course. He recorded himself engaged in ordinary tasks about his house and garden, sweeping his barn, fitting a cistern for his fountain, and weeding and raking his melons (5–7/46). In one entry in this volume he looked back at the past years and asked himself, "Why hast thou mourned so long, and for the last five or six years folded thy hands in sadness, or put them forth to do what thou wouldst not, or what thou didst deem thyself desperate to undertake? Ah was it that the world was not heaven and none would join thee to make it such?" (3/16/46). Alcott still feared that nature would be his only audience, but in the years to come an older, milder Bronson Alcott would command attention and respect (7/4/46).

Just as Emerson finally came to accept the restrictions of fate on the scope of self-reliance, so Alcott came to accept the fact that there were limits that could not be passed. In his essay on "Fate" Emerson argued that failing in our "hope to reform men. . . . we find we must begin earlier,—at school. But the boys and girls are not docile. We decide they are not of good stock. We must begin our reform earlier still,— at generation: that is to say, there is Fate, or laws of the world." Alcott expressed the same idea in his diary: "I once thought all minds in childhood much the same and that education lay in the power of calling these forth in something of a common accomplishment. But now I see that character is more of a nature than of acquirement" (3/undated/46). This was an especially significant admission, since Alcott's career had been as an educator, and he had dedicated himself to proving that, as humans were most easily manipulated during childhood, the school was an ideal place for human reform.

Alcott continued to write in his journals after 1846. Indeed, he continued to keep a diary for another quarter century, amassing a considerable volume of material. But the Alcott of these years seems a very different man from the diarist of the earlier period, and his journals seem to be part of a very different work. They lack some of the vitality of the earlier volumes. Alcott seems to have traded some of his hope for serenity. He wrote of walks through nature with Thoreau and Emerson, and the later diary has numerous entries detailing his involvement with these and other famous writers and thinkers. However, he had changed. As he admitted in his diary, "I am not as once I was. I am become recluse and thoughtful in the extreme, and an idealist, from having been a socialist and sentimentalist as extreme in days past. . . . I have accepted and submitted against long-cherished hopes and endeavors, seeing it must be so" (3/20/50).

Although he claimed to have become more involved in the ideal than the material, Alcott had really rejected only his attempt at social reform, and that only partially. Aroused by a cause, he might still throw himself into some activity. However, in both his public and his private lives he became more rather than less interested in practical results. He also became so practical and moderate, at least by the standards of his earlier life, that in 1853 he was invited to conduct his "Conversations" at the Harvard Divinity School from which Emerson had been excluded since the controversy surrounding his "Address." This invitation was just one sign of Alcott's increasing orthodoxy in religious and other matters.

In his new pursuit of the practical Alcott even began to question his own journalizing. In one entry he even complained that the diary was "taking the best of my time" but had not produced practical results. It was too private a form even to serve as an aid in writing an autobiography: "I should be happy if I had before me the transcript of a single day. But the best refuses to be put into a pillory of words, and to be gazed at, as multitudes stare at culprits, and mock, in the marketplace." Alcott complained that although a diary might be "the most difficult feat of authorship," he could not stop writing, "I write, write, driven by a demon with the quill behind his ear—eloquent of a morning, always in praise of ink; then tempting me of afternoons to silence and depose him, as Luther did, by dashing the contents of my standish into his face for riddance of him once and forever" (1/12/51).

Always, the perfect, the complete entry eluded him. Alcott also treated this problem in the first entry of *Concord Days,* a work written in diary form and drawn to a large extent from his diary. He wrote that although his journal taught him a great deal, including "whatever skill I possess with the pen," it had not allowed him to capture fully even one day: "Could I succeed in sketching to the life a single day's doings, [I] should esteem myself as having accomplished the chiefest feat in literature. Yet the nobler the life and the busier, the less perhaps gets written."[31] The converse of Alcott's comments here is supported by the fact that his diary seems to have declined in proportion with the growing public acceptance of his "Conversations" and other lectures.

Another sign of Alcott's new interest in connecting his speculations to "facts" is evident in an entry written as part of his reaction to Carlyle's *Memoirs*. The entry shows how Alcott had been reevaluating his own life and work. Declaring that while Carlyle had ridiculed him as "a sentimentalist," unable to support his "dream amidst his wild whirl of words," Alcott explained that the reason for his reticence was that his own mysticism was "a less muscular type" than Carlyle's and that "at a later period" he could have "shown how firmly . . . [he] was anchored in facts and knew their place" (8/21/81).

Aging, Alcott declined to look toward the afterlife. Instead, following Thoreau's lead, he tried to concern himself with "one world at a time" (9/17/82). Even so, the journals for 1882 show his growing recognition that the world he had known was passing if it had not already passed. In March he noted Longfellow's death, which left Holmes, Whittier, and Lowell as the only "elder poets" surviving; in April Emerson died, leaving Alcott as one of the few remaining early proponents of American Transcendentalism (3/24/82, 4/28/82, 6/16/82). Traveling to his childhood home, he found, "The homes are mostly deserted, or inhabited by strangers. The fields where I ploughed, meadows where I swung the scythe, orchards where I harvested, are grown up in sweet-fern, barren, unfenced, and all gone to ruin" (9/30/82). Perceptions seemed clearer "with closed eyes" than through the senses (5/11–13/82). Though he would live over five years longer, he wrote his last entry in October 1882.

Chapter Seven
Conclusion

While the half century mark is a convenient point to terminate this study, the development of lives and nations rarely divides so evenly. A number of diaries that have their bulk or their most significant entries in the second half of the nineteenth century had their origin in the period we have been considering. Among these are Hawthorne's *Notebooks* and Charles Francis Adams's *Diaries*.

There are some differences in the types and numbers of diaries written after 1849. One obvious difference is in the number of exploration diaries, a situation that resulted from the gradual disappearance of the wilderness as the frontier became settled. However, most of the same diary forms written earlier continued to be written in substantial numbers: travel diaries such as that of Herman Melville, diplomatic diaries such as those of Benjamin Moran and George Mifflin Dallas, Transcendentalist journals such as that of Henry David Thoreau. In some cases old forms were modified. For example, Alice James's diary of her final illness does not focus on God the way that of Samuel Cole Davis does; and yet it is related to the type of spiritual journal he wrote.

At the end of the period covered in this study America was on the verge of some of her greatest achievements and some of her worst agonies. As in the past, American diaries would continue to chronicle such events of national importance even as they recorded the personal victories and defeats of their authors. Early diaries such as those of Anne Home Livingston and Margaret Dwight Bell focus on the roles and treatment of women. The rising consciousness that is part of the women's movement became more highly developed in later diaries such as those of Ruth Benedict and Sylvia Plath.

As diaries are often created in response to disturbances or dislocations in the lives of their authors, it should not seem surprising that the most distinct and significant group of American diaries written during the last half of the nineteenth century are those dealing with the Civil War. In the first half of the century America had experienced two declared wars and numerous conflicts with Indian tribes; however, none of these compared in scope or effect to the Civil War. One has only to go to any library and view the number of works both factual and fictional about that war to recognize that it holds, and has long held, a special place in the American consciousness.

It did not require the passage of time for Americans to recognize the heroic and tragic implications of the Civil War. As the diary literature of this period attests, Americans almost immediately perceived that this war would be one that would have a major effect on their world. Some of these diaries were written by soldiers, such as John Beatty, a Union officer, and John L. Ransom, a prisoner at Andersonville. The most distinguished group of diaries was written by Southern women: Eliza Francis Andrews, Mary Boykin Chesnut,[1] Sarah Morgan Dawson, Katherine Stone Holmes, and Judith McGuire.

Another important group of American diarists were professional writers. While throughout America's history a large percentage of her authors have kept diaries, those of the last century have been especially conscious of the form. Among the writers who kept important diaries are Theodore Dreiser and F. Scott Fitzgerald. Earlier writers like Emerson recognized the importance of their diaries to their published works, but they did not think to publish the actual diaries during their lifetimes. The case is different with a number of later writers, such as John Steinbeck and Allen Ginsberg.

Americans have also continued to write life diaries, preserving for the future both their own personalities and their particular perspectives on their times. Among the best of those written in the last half of the nineteenth century are the works of Richard Henry Dana, Sidney George Fisher, and George Templeton Strong. Because diaries of this kind are often highly personal, the best twentieth-century diaries may not be publicly known until well into the twenty-first century.

When we read these diaries we come not only to understand the specific experiences and attitudes of their authors, but also our own. Even when we view a diary's world secondhand, its events can become part of our own experience; and, in those instances in which a diary has been sufficiently developed to have its own distinct identity, its created personality can become a friend.

Notes and References

Chapter One

1. For a more complete treatment of colonial American diaries see Steven E. Kagle, *American Diary Literature 1607–1800,* Twayne's United States Authors Series 342 (Boston, 1979).
2. *A Gentleman's Progress: The Itinerarium of Dr. Alexander Hamilton,* ed. Carl Bridenbaugh (Chapel Hill, 1948), 199.

Chapter Two

1. *The Diary of Samuel Cole Davis,* from a modernized typescript of the manuscript in the Quaker Collection of the Haverford College Library, entries for 9/18–19/08. Hereafter references to Davis's diary are cited by entry date in the text.
2. The term "belief voice" refers to a spiritual vision. The occurrence of such visitations is in keeping with Quaker beliefs and figure in John Woolman's journal. This vision is only one of several noted in Davis's journal.
3. This entry is dated 4/1/08, but it was probably written the next day April 2.
4. Autobiographical insert following the entry for 2/25/09.
5. *Journal of that Faithful Servant of Christ, Charles Osborn* (Cincinnati, 1854), 1–4. Hereafter page references to this edition are cited in parentheses in the text.
6. It need not take away from the validity of Osborn's experiences to note that modern medicine tends to ascribe such alternating periods of depression and elation to psychological or physiological causes. These depressions were not part of some passing phase; he continued to mention periods in which "Darkness seemed to hover around me, and weigh down my spirit" in some of the later journal entries (407).
7. It may be significant that the manuscript covering more than a month of the period before and including the beginning of his visit to Philadelphia is missing.
8. At the time Osborn's home was in Economy, Indiana.
9. Included in the volume in which Osborn's journal was printed is the text of a pamphlet he wrote that was probably published about 1850. See 417–60.
10. *Memoirs of Catherine Seely* (New York, 1843), 33–34. Hereafter page references to this edition are cited in parentheses in the text.

11. *Memoranda and Correspondence of Mildred Ratcliff* (Philadelphia, 1890), 82. Hereafter page references to this edition are cited in parentheses in the text.

Chapter Three

1. For an examination of this idea in the literature of the early nineteenth century, see my introduction to *America: Exploration and Travel,* ed. Steven E. Kagle (Bowling Green, 1979), 3–7.

2. The records of Sergeant Nathaniel Pryor and Private Robert Frazier have not been located. There is also a possibility that Private George Shannon kept a diary. See the introduction to *The Original Journals of the Lewis and Clark Expedition 1804–1806,* ed. Ruben Gold Thwaites (New York, 1904–1905), 1:xxxiv. Further references to this edition are cited in parentheses in the text.

3. Scholars seeking to preserve historical accuracy will wish to use the individual diaries, most of which appear in the edition edited by Ruben Gold Thwaites. For non-scholarly use one may choose from the many editions of Biddle's version or Bernard De Voto's abridgment of the originals published in Thwaites's edition; both preserve the essential sense of the diary form.

4. Zebulon Pike, *Journals of Zebulon Montgomery Pike,* ed. Donald Jackson (Norman, Okla., 1966), 1:361–62. The journals are all printed in the first volume of this two-volume work. Hereafter page references to that volume are cited in parentheses in the text.

5. *Narrative Journal of Travels* (Albany, 1821) reprinted as *Travels through the Northwest Regions of the United States* (Ann Arbor, 1966), xii; an excellent new edition of this is *Narrative Journal of Travels through the NorthWestern Regions of the United States Extending from Detroit through the Great Chain of American Lakes to the Sources of the Mississippi River in the Year 1820,* ed. Mentor L. Williams (East Lansing, Mich., 1953). Other diaries by Schoolcraft include *A View of the Lead Mines of Missouri* (New York, 1819), other versions of which were published under the titles *Scenes and Adventures in the Semi-Alpine Region of the Ozark Mountains* (Philadelphia, 1853) and *Schoolcraft in the Ozarks,* ed. Hugh Park (Van Buren, Ark., 1955)—a reprint of *Journal of a Tour into the Interior of Missouri and Arkansas in 1818 and 1819* (London, 1821); *Travels in the Central Portions of the Mississippi Valley* (New York, 1825). Diary material from the period after 1821 is included in *Personal Memoirs of a Residence of Thirty Years with the Indian Tribes on the American Frontier* (Philadelphia, 1851). This nondated introduction appears on p. xii of Williams's edition. Because of the fragmented publication of Schoolcraft's diaries and the problems some readers may have in gaining access to particular editions, references to Schoolcraft's diary entries are by entry date rather than by work and page number and appear in parentheses in the text.

6. Philip P. Mason, "Introduction" to Henry R. Schoolcraft, *The Lit-*

erary Voyager or Muzzeniegun, ed. Philip P. Mason (East Lansing, Mich., 1962), xvi.

7. For the quotations in context, compare Schoolcraft's diary (225) and that of Baron Louis Armand La Hontan, *New Voyage to North America,* ed. Ruben Gold Thwaites (Chicago, 1905), 2:421.

8. "Transallegania or the Groans of Missouri, A Poem," in *Schoolcraft in the Ozarks,* 173–75.

9. Mason, "Introduction," *Literary Voyager,* xvii–xxvi.

10. Material on Frémont's later explorations appears in John Charles Frémont, *Memoirs of My Life* (Chicago, 1887), some parts of which are in diary form. Accounts of Frémont's first, second, and fourth expeditions were also recorded in the German language diaries of Frémont's second in command and cartographer, Charles Preuss (1803–1854). See note 12 below.

11. John Charles Frémont, *The Expeditions of John Charles Frémont,* ed. Donald Jackson and Mary Lee Spence (Urbana, Ill., 1970), 1:185. Hereafter volume and page references to this edition are cited in parentheses in the text.

12. Charles Preuss, *Exploring with Frémont,* trans. and ed. Erwin G. Gudde and Elisabeth K. Gudde (Norman, Okla., 1958), 127–28. Part of this passage is cited in Jackson and Spence's edition of Frémont's writings (681).

13. Jackson and Spence (270) note that this summit was probably Woodrow Wilson Peak (slightly north of Gannet Peak), which at 13,804 ft. is the highest point in Wyoming.

14. Mrs. Bell's ancestry provides an interesting set of coincidental relationships. She was not only the great-granddaughter of Jonathan Edwards, but she was also the niece of Timothy Dwight whose travel journals were later rewritten and published in epistolary form. See Timothy Dwight, *Travels in New England and New York* (Cambridge, Mass., 1969).

15. Margaret Van Horn Dwight Bell, *A Journey to Ohio in 1810,* ed. Max Farrand (New Haven, 1912), 64. Hereafter page references appear in parentheses in the text.

16. *The Journals of Francis Parkman,* ed. Mason Wade (New York, 1947), 1:31. Hereafter volume and page references appear in parentheses in the text.

17. "Editor's Introduction," Francis Parkman, *The Oregon Trail,* ed. E. N. Feltskog (Madison, Wis., 1969), 30a.

18. The Donner party was a group of western emigrants who, attempting to reach California via a route across the Sierras, became trapped by snows and forced to resort to cannibalism so that some might survive.

19. Irving often wrote his notebook entries in pencil on "tiny artists' sketchpads," while he used ink and larger-sized manuscript books for his dated diary entries. See "Introduction," *The Complete Works of Washington Irving: Journals and Notebooks: Volume II, 1807–1822,* ed. Walter A. Reichart and Lillian Schlissel (Boston, 1981), xvii–xviii.

20. Ibid., 141, 147. This volume is part of what will be a five-volume Center for Editions of American Authors approved edition. Where possible,

references to Irving's journals and notebooks will be to this edition and volume and page numbers will be cited in parentheses in the text. For portions of Irving's diaries not yet published in this edition, references will be to *The Journals of Washington Irving,* ed. William P. Trent and George S. Hellman (Boston, 1919), reprinted by Haskell House Publishers, 1970. References to this edition will be designated in the text as *T,* followed by volume and page number.

21. Reichart and Schlissel in their "Introduction" noted Irving's belief in a commonality of purpose between "the landscape painter and the writer." They also claimed that Irving's "descriptions, even when brief, followed a pattern: first the distant scene and the faraway images; then the scene closer with its details . . . lastly the sounds." I find their argument useful, especially its analysis of the divisions in Irving's observations, but would suggest that Irving's ordering of these divisions is not as pervasive as they have argued (2:xi, xix).

22. The extant diaries for Irving's first European trip were written in 1804–1805; those for the latter period cover only two brief sections in the years 1815 and 1817 and a longer and more complete journal during the years 1820–1827. Some of the balance of Irving's accounts of these stays in Europe is in notebook form.

23. Washington Irving, *A Tour on the Prairies,* ed. John Francis McDermott (Norman, Okla., 1956), 53.

24. In addition to the published diaries, there are some surviving portions of Audubon's diaries from the period 1822–1824. Maria Audubon in her edition of her grandfather's diaries wrote that this section describes a period of poverty and mental suffering which can show "the very heart of the man who wrote it"; unfortunately, except for brief excerpts, she considered this material "too sacred" for publication in her edition, and no more has been published. Some portions of the diary manuscript are in the library of the American Philosophical Society; some are in private collections.

25. John James Audubon, *Audubon in His Journals,* ed. Maria Audubon (New York, 1897), 1:460, reprinted by Dover Publications, 1960. While this work includes most of Audubon's best series of diaries and is the only published version of much of Audubon's record, it is too heavily altered to be relied on. Some of the extant diaries were published in two rare editions: *The Journal of John James Audubon Made During His Trip to New Orleans in 1820–1821,* ed. Howard Corning (Boston, 1929), and *The Journal of John James Audubon Made While Obtaining Subscriptions to His Birds of America 1840–1843,* ed. Howard Corning (Boston, 1929). An excellent edition of the first year of Audubon's 1826–1829 diary was published as *The 1826 Journal Of John James Audubon,* transcribed with an introduction and notes by Alice Ford (Norman, Okla., 1967). Hereafter all references to the 1826 diary are to Ford's edition and are cited in the text as *F,* followed by page number. The references to Maria Audubon's edition are cited as *A,* followed by volume and page number.

26. Frances Anne Kemble, *Journal of a Residence in America* (London, 1835), 1:1. Hereafter page references are to this edition and appear in parentheses in the text.

27. One entry, for which she later apologized, dealt with a dinner at the home of Philip Hone (whose diary is treated in Chapter Five). In it she called the American guests "aborigines" for "paring" their peaches "like so many potatoes" (1:106).

28. "Editor's Introduction," Frances Anne Kemble, *Residence on a Georgia Plantation 1838–1839,* ed. John A. Scott (New York, 1961), xxxv; hereafter page references to this edition are cited in parentheses in the text.

29. Published anonymously, *Journal of a Tour in Italy in the Year 1821* (New York, 1824) is generally credited to Theodore Dwight (1796–1866), but it is sometimes listed as having been written with the assistance of William Darby. The extremely long and well-written entries (one entry covering two days runs over 12,000 words) seem to have been extensively revised for publication. Hereafter page references to this edition are cited in parentheses in the text.

30. Unfortunately there is no good edition of Cole's diaries. His record is most easily found embedded in Louis Legrand Noble, *The Life and Works of Thomas Cole,* ed. Elliot S. Vesell (Cambridge, Mass., 1964). Vesell notes in his edition that Noble not only published only portions of Cole's diary but also that Noble even significantly altered some of the original entries he reproduced, 94; hereafter page references to this edition are cited in the text. However, for extensive or detailed use scholars should consult the manuscript at the New York Historical Society or the microfilm copy available at the Detroit Art Institute.

Chapter Four

1. The treaty ending the War of 1812 was signed on December 24, 1814.

2. *The Diary of James Gallatin,* ed. Count Gallatin (New York, 1916), 25. Hereafter page references to this work are cited in parentheses in the text.

3. Madame De Staël: Anne-Louise-Germaine Necker de Staël (1766–1817). She is most famous for her Paris salon and her writings.

4. *Grisette* is used here as a euphemism for *prostitute* or *courtesan.* The word, which first meant shop girl, has its origin in *gris,* the French word for gray, the color worn by milliners.

5. Of course, unlike Morris, who was American ambassador during the French Revolution, Gallatin had little interest in diplomatic activity. See Governeur Morris, *Diary and Letters of Governeur Morris,* ed. Anne C. Morris, 2 vols. (New York, 1888), and Kagle, *American Diary Literature 1607–1800,* 75–81.

6. *The Diary of James K. Polk,* ed. Milo M. Quaife (Chicago, 1910), 2:100–1. Hereafter references to this edition are cited in parentheses in the text.

7. In another entry about a year later one of Benton's sons swore "profanely" at Polk when a demand for a military commission was denied (3:202–3).

8. See Allan Nevins, "Introduction and Notes," *Polk: The Diary of a President 1845–1849,* ed. Allan Nevins (New York, 1929), 12.

9. This is not the only example in the diary of Buchanan's vacillations. In other entries Polk described the way Buchanan totally reversed his position on the Oregon boundary line and on territorial acquisitions from the Mexican War.

Chapter Five

1. Allan Nevins, "Introduction" in *The Diary of Philip Hone 1828–1851,* ed. Allan Nevins (New York, 1927), 1:vi–xx. In his edition, the most complete version published, Alan Nevins expressed his conviction that he had included "virtually everything in the original manuscript that is of value to the student or general reader," and certainly this version is sufficient for most purposes; but it is far from complete, containing only a third of the material in the manuscript in the New York Historical Society library (1:vi, 1). Nevins even omitted some interesting entries in the earlier edition of Bayard Tuckerman; therefore, while most references in this section are to Nevins's edition, some are to Tuckerman's and these are cited in the text as *T,* followed by page number.

2. It is interesting to note that three of these five themselves kept significant diaries. Other important diarists mentioned in Hone's record include Cole, Dallas, Dunlap, Emerson, Kemble, Polk, Schoolcraft, and Ticknor.

3. At present the only relatively complete edition of the diary is *Memoirs of John Quincy Adams, Comprising Portions of his Diary from 1795 to 1848,* ed. Charles Francis Adams (Philadelphia, 1874–1877). This edition with its twelve large volumes is substantial; yet even that version includes only "portions" of the diary, omitting many sections such as that covering the first fifteen years of the work. Entries during the period 1787–1789 were published under the title *Life in a New England Town,* ed. Charles Francis Adams, Jr. (Boston, 1903). The complete diary will eventually be published as a part of the Adams Papers. At present only two volumes have appeared, *Diary of John Quincy Adams,* ed. David Grayson Allen, Robert J. Taylor, Marc Friedlaender, and Celeste Walker (Cambridge, Mass., 1981). These volumes cover the period 1779–1788. All citations from Adams's diary will refer to these editions. References to the *Memoirs* will be cited by volume and page number in parentheses in the text. References to *Life in a New England Town* are cited in the text as *L,* followed by page number.

4. Note: Bayard, Russell, and Gallatin's son James (See Chapter Four) also kept diaries though not all deal with this period of negotiations.

5. Louisa Catherine Adams's diaries and those of other members of the family are available on a microfilm edition of the manuscript. The manuscript is located at the Massachusetts Historical Society, but microfilm copies are at several libraries. The microfilm diary is part of *The Adams Papers* (Boston, 1954).

Chapter Six

1. Joel Porte, ed., *Emerson in His Journals* (Cambridge, 1982), 3.

2. The bulk of Thoreau's journals was written after 1850 and will be treated in a later number in this series.

3. *The Journals and Miscellaneous Notebooks of Ralph Waldo Emerson*, ed. William H. Gilman et al. (Cambridge, Mass., 1960), 1:215. Hereafter references to this edition are cited by volume and page number in parentheses in the text.

4. See for example the ballads about knights, castles, dragons, and witches (1:103–7) and fables about giants and musical trees (1:114; 2:29–30).

5. "Wide World No. 4" was dedicated to the dead, No. 6 to "the force which shall reveal Nature to Man," No. 7 to the "Spirit of America," No. 8 to the slave, and No. 9 to the future and its progress. The practice ended with the dedication of No. 10 to Eloquence (1:91, 115; 2:3, 40–42, 75–77, 105). Also note that No. 5 and No. 14 are missing.

6. 2:273. See also editor's notes 2:112, 273.

7. See editor's foreword 3:ix.

8. As the editors of the *Journals* suggest in their foreword to volume 9, the day of Emerson's departure seems to prefigure Ishmael's voyage in *Moby-Dick* (4:xii).

9. During this period alone he notes reading published diaries such as Kemble's and manuscript diaries including Alcott's (5:83, 167, 170).

10. *Nature*, in *The Collected Works of Ralph Waldo Emerson: Volume One, Nature, Addresses and Other Lectures*, ed. Alfred R. Ferguson (Cambridge, Mass., 1979), 8.

11. "Self-Reliance," in *The Collected Works of Ralph Waldo Emerson: Volume Two, Essays First Series*, ed. Alfred R. Ferguson and Jean Ferguson Carr (Cambridge, Mass., 1979), 30. Further references to "Self-Reliance" are to this edition.

12. Vol. 5:216. This entry was made on the eve of the seventh anniversary of Emerson's marriage to Ellen.

13. The editors of the *Journals* stated that "Emerson had early realized that as a public preacher and lecturer he would be only as good as his journals were," and so attempted to make them into an "artificial memory" (7:xvi). Such a memory involved connections that transcended the temporal sequence of the diary form.

14. Of course, this idea did not even originate with Emerson, whose position was to a great extent a secularization of the principle of divinely ordained callings so important to his Puritan ancestors.

15. Thoreau later used parts of his position in both "Walking" and *Walden*.

16. "Self-Reliance," 44.

17. Henry David Thoreau, *Walden*, ed. J. Lyndon Shanley (Princeton, 1971), 268–69.

18. Ever since the success of her novels, Louisa May Alcott's fame has eclipsed that of her father; indeed, one of the major biographies of Alcott was titled *The Father of Little Women*.

19. No edition of Alcott's complete works was ever published and except for excerpts and anthology selections few individual titles remain in print.

20. Emerson, *Journals*, 5:98–99.

21. *The Journals of Bronson Alcott*, ed. Odell Shepard (Boston, 1938). Some sections have been published in their entirety; see bibliography. The manuscripts of the Alcott journals are in the Houghton Library, Harvard University, but they are owned by the Concord Public Library, which holds a microfilm copy. Given these multiple sources, references to Alcott's journal will be made by entry date in parentheses in the text. Where possible I have used examples that can be read in context in published versions, but have corrected all texts as necessary to agree with the manuscript. Manuscript used by permission of the Houghton Library.

22. Shepard, "Introduction," *Journals of Bronson Alcott*, xiv–xv.

23. A manuscript volume entitled *Autobiography* in the Houghton Library.

24. (8/28/35) It seems likely that Shepard was referring to this passage when he suggested that Alcott directed the diary to "his own future self" that he might "catch some hint of a total tendency and character" and so find how his life had been "emblematic . . . of ultimate truth." Shepard, *Journals of Bronson Alcott*, 1:xiii–xiv.

25. (4/18/31) This idea and language were not original with Alcott. In his introduction to his manuscript *History of an Infant* Alcott quoted an almost identical statement by another American educator, William Shields Reid (1778–1853).

26. Shepard calls this year for Alcott the "seedtime of his mind" (1:34).

27. In a letter to his mother written on March 18, 1839, Alcott wrote:

I am full of hope, and everything looks encouraging. . . . I have many friends and am making more daily, and have only to be true to my principles, to get not only a useful name, but bread, and shelter, and raiment. A few years more and I shall reap even these secondary rewards, and be above want. . . . I am still the same Hoper that I have always been. . . .

A young Hoper is on his way. . . . I am to have a Boy. In *The Letters of A. Bronson Alcott,* ed. Richard L. Herrnstadt (Ames, Iowa, 1969), 42.

28. Madelon Bedell, *The Alcotts* (New York, 1980), 154.

29. Frederick Dahlstrand, "Bronson Alcott," in *The Transcendentalists* ed. Joel Myerson, (New York, 1984), 88, wrote that "Alcott lost the volumes . . . when a stagecoach rumbled off with his baggage."

30. Cited by Shepard (1:171) as January/undated/46.

31. A. Bronson Alcott, *Concord Days* (Boston, 1872), 3–4.

Chapter Seven

1. Mary Boykin Chesnut's *Diary from Dixie* is not actually a true diary, but rather a re-creation of her diary of the period.

Selected Bibliography

PRIMARY SOURCES

1. American Diaries of the First Half of the Nineteenth Century
Adams, Charles Francis. *Diary of Charles Francis Adams.* Edited by Aïda Di
Pace Donald and David Donald. Cambridge: Belknap Press, 1964. It
has taken two decades for the publication of the first six volumes covering
the period from 1820 to 1836 (the diary continues until 1880); therefore,
it is unlikely that the work will be completed for many years. Fortunately, the manuscript diary at the Massachusetts Historical Society is
available on microfilm with other portions of the Adams Papers at many
major libraries.
Adams, John Quincy. *Diary of John Quincy Adams.* Edited by David Grayson
Allen, Robert J. Taylor, Marc Friedlaender, and Celeste Walker. Cambridge: Belknap Press, 1981. When completed as part of the Adams
Papers Series, this edition will become the standard. The first two volumes were published in 1981, but it is unlikely that the work will be
completed for many years. These volumes cover the period from 1779 to
1788, earlier than that in the editions below.
————. *Life in a New England Town.* Edited by Charles Francis Adams, Jr.
Boston: Little Brown & Co., 1903. Covers the period from 1787 to
1789.
————. *Memoirs of John Quincy Adams, Comprising Portions of his Diary from
1795 to 1848.* Edited by Charles Francis Adams. 12 vols. Philadelphia:
Lippincott, 1874–1877. Presently the only relatively complete version
of Adams's diary, this edition covers the period from 1794 to 1848.
Adams, Louisa Catherine. *Diary of Louisa Catherine Adams. The Adams Papers.*
Boston: Massachusetts Historical Society, 1954.
Alcott, A. Bronson. *The Journals of Bronson Alcott.* 2 vols. Edited by Odell
Shepard. Boston: Little Brown, 1938. Reprint. Port Washington, N.Y.:
Kennikat Press, 1966. Excerpts from extant journals. The text contains
several minor errors.
————. "Bronson Alcott's 'Journal for 1836.'". Edited by Joel Myerson.
Studies in the American Renaissance, 1978: 17–104.
————. "Bronson Alcott's 'Journal for 1837.'" Edited by Larry A. Carlson.
Studies in the American Renaissance, 1980, 1981: 27–132, 53–168.
————. "Bronson Alcott's 'Scripture for 1840.'" Edited by Joel Myerson.

Emerson Society Quarterly 20 (1974): 236–59. Contains part of diary for 1840.

———. Manuscript Journals. 54 vols. In the Alcott Pratt Collection of the Houghton Library, Harvard University, Cambridge, Mass. These are owned by the Concord Public Library, Concord, Mass., which also has a microfilm copy.

Alcott, Anna. "Anna Alcott's Diary at Fruitlands." In *Bronson Alcott's Fruitlands.* Edited by Clara Endicott Sears. Boston: Houghton Mifflin, 1915, 86–105.

Alcott, Louisa May. "Louisa May Alcott's Diary at Fruitlands." In *Bronson Alcott's Fruitlands.* Edited by Clara Endicott Sears. Boston: Houghton Mifflin, 1915, 106–11.

Audubon, John James. *Audubon in His Journals.* Edited by Maria R. Audubon. 2 vols. New York: Charles Scribner's Sons, 1897. Reprint. New York: Dover Publications, 1960. The only published version of some of Audubon's diaries; unfortunately, Maria Audubon so altered the original text that this edition is highly unreliable.

———. *The 1826 Journal of John James Audubon.* Transcribed with an introduction and notes by Alice Ford. Norman: University of Oklahoma Press, 1967. A fine edition of the first part of Audubon's diary of a trip to Europe.

———. *The Journal of John James Audubon Made During His Trip to New Orleans in 1820–1821.* Edited by Howard Corning. Boston: Club of Odd Volumes, 1929.

———. *The Journal of John James Audubon Made While Obtaining Subscriptions to His Birds of America 1840–1843.* Edited by Howard Corning. Boston: Club of Odd Volumes, 1929. Travels in New York, New England, and Canada.

Bayard, James Asheton. "Diaries" in *Papers of James A. Bayard. American Historical Association Annual Report* 2 (1913): 385–516. Bayard's travel diary includes entries on the period in which he was, with John Quincy Adams, one of the commissioners negotiating the Treaty of Ghent.

Bell, John R. *The Journal of Captain John R. Bell Official Journalist for the Stephen H. Long Expedition to the Rocky Mountains in 1820.* Edited by Harlin M. Fuller and LeRoy R. Hafen. Glendale: Arthur H. Clark Co., 1957.

Bell, Margaret van Horn Dwight. *A Journey to Ohio in 1810.* Edited by Max Farrand. New Haven: Yale University Press, 1912.

Clark, William, and Meriwether Lewis. *The Original Journals of the Lewis and Clark Expedition 1804–1806.* Edited by Ruben Gold Thwaites. 8 vols. New York: Dodd Mead, 1904–1905.

Cole, Thomas. *Journals.* In manuscript at the New York Historical Society or the microfilm copy available at the Detroit Art Institute. Excerpts are included in Louis Legrand Noble, *The Life and Works of Thomas Cole*. See citation for Noble below under Secondary Sources.

Cooper, James Fenimore. *Letters and Journals of James Fenimore Cooper*. Edited by James Franklin Beard. 6 vols. Cambridge: Belknap Press, 1960. Interesting travel diaries, although weaker than those discussed at length in this volume.

Davis, Samuel Cole. *Diary of Samuel Cole Davis*. Manuscript in the Quaker Collection of the Haverford College Library. Haverford, Pa. An edition for publication is in progress.

Dunlap, William. *Diary of William Dunlap (1766–1839): The Memoirs of a Dramatist, Theatrical Manager, Painter, Critic, Novelist and Historian*. Edited by Dorothy C. Barck. New York Historical Society Collections. Vols. 62–64. New York: New York Historical Society, 1930. Reprint. 3 vols. New York: B. Blom, 1969. The intrinsic literary value of this extensive diary (1786–1834) is marred by gaps and fragmentary entries. However, Dunlap's place as an American painter and playwright and his relationships with other important diarists make this diary worthy of consideration.

Dwight, Theodore, Jr. *A Journal of a Tour in Italy in the Year 1821*. New York: Abraham Paul, 1824. On the title page the author is listed only as "An American," but the diary is generally credited to Dwight, sometimes with the assistance of William Darby.

Emerson, Ralph Waldo. *The Journals and Miscellaneous Notebooks of Ralph Waldo Emerson*. Edited by William H. Gilman, Alfred R. Ferguson, George P. Clark, and Merrell R. Davis. 16 vols. Cambridge: Belknap Press, 1960–1982.

———. *Emerson in His Journals*. Edited by Joel Porte. Cambridge: Belknap Press, 1982. A useful selection from Emerson's long diary.

Frémont, Johon C. *The Expeditions of John Charles Frémont*. Edited by Donald Jackson and Mary Lee Spence. 2 vols. Urbana: University of Illinois Press, 1970. The diary is in volume one.

———. *Memoirs of My Life Including the Narrative Five Journeys of Western Exploration During the Years 1842, 1843–4, 1845–6–7, 1853–4*. Chicago: Belford, Clarke, 1887. Contains some parts written in diary form as well as additional biographical material.

———. *Report of the Exploring Expedition to the Rocky Mountains in the Year 1842, and to Oregon and Northern California in the Years 1843–'44* Washington, D.C.: Gales and Seaton Printers, 1845. Reprint. Ann Arbor: University Microfilms, 1966.

Fuller, Margaret. *See Ossoli*.

Gallatin, James. *The Diary of James Gallatin, Secretary to Albert Gallatin A Great Peacemaker 1813–1827*. Edited by Count James Francis Gallatin. New York: Charles Scribner's Sons, 1916. Reprint. Westport, Conn.: Greenwood Press, 1979.

Gass, Patrick. *Gass's Journal of the Lewis and Clark Expedition.* Edited by James K. Hosmer. Chicago: A. C. McClurg, 1904. Heavily revised for publication.

Hone, Philip. *The Diary of Philip Hone.* Edited by Bayard Tuckerman. 2 vols. New York: Dodd Mead, 1899.

————. *The Diary of Philip Hone 1828–1851.* Edited by Allan Nevins. 2 vols. New York: Dodd, Mead, 1927. Reprint. New York: Kraus Reprint Co., 1969. This edition is sufficient for most readers; though this is the most complete version of Hone's diary published, it contains only a third of the material in the manuscript in the New York Historical Society library.

Irving, Washington. *The Complete Works of Washington Irving: Journals and Notebooks: Volume I, 1803–1806.* Edited by Nathalia Wright. Boston: Twayne Publishers, 1969.

————. *The Complete Works of Washington Irving: Journals and Notebooks: Volume II, 1807–1822.* Edited by Walter A. Reichart and Lillian Schlissel. Boston: Twayne Publishers, 1981.

————. *The Complete Works of Washington Irving: Journals and Notebooks: Volume III, 1819–1827.* Edited by Walter A. Reichart. Boston: Twayne Publishers, 1970.

————. *The Journals of Washington Irving.* Edited by W. P. Trent and G. S. Williams. 3 vols. Boston: Bibliophile Society, 1919. Reprint. New York: Haskell House, 1970.

Kemble, Frances Anne (Fanny). *Journal of a Residence in America.* 2 vols. London: John Murray, 1835.

————. *Residence on a Georgia Plantation 1838–1839.* Edited by John A. Scott. New York: Alfred Knopf, 1961.

Lewis, Meriwether. See: Clark, William.

Nuttall, Thomas. *A Journal of Travels into the Arkansas Territory During the Year 1819.* Edited by Savoie Lottinville. Norman: University of Oklahoma Press, 1980.

————. *Nuttall's Travels into the Old Northwest, An Unpublished 1810 Diary.* Edited by Jeannette E. Graustein. *Chronica Botanica* 14, nos. 1 and 2.

Ordway, John. "Journals" in *The Journals of Captain Meriwether Lewis and Sergant John Ordway, Kept on the Expedition of Western Exploration 1803–1806.* Edited by Milo M. Quaife. *Wisconsin Historical Society Publications* 22 (1916): 79-402.

Osborn, Charles. *Journal of that Faithful Servant of Christ, Charles Osborne Containing an Account of Many of His Travels and Labors in the Work of the Ministry, and His Trials and Exercises in the Service of the Lord and in Defense of the Truth as It Is in Jesus.* Cincinnati: Achilles Pugh, 1854.

Ossoli, Margaret Fuller, Marchioness. *Memoirs of Margaret Fuller Ossoli.* Edited by Ralph Waldo Emerson, William Channing, and James Freeman Clarke. 2 vols. Boston: Philips Sampson, 1852.

Parkman, Francis. *The Journals of Francis Parkman*. Edited by Mason Wade. New York: Harper & Brothers, 1947. 2 vols.

Pike, Zebulon. *Journals of Zebulon Montgomery Pike*. Edited by Donald Jackson. 2 vols. Norman: University of Oklahoma Press, 1966. The diary is in the first volume.

Polk, James K. *The Diary of James K. Polk*. Edited by Milo M. Quaife. 4 vols. Chicago: A. C. McClurg & Co., 1910.

————. *Polk: The Diary of a President 1845–1849*. Edited by Allan Nevins. New York: Longmans Green, 1929. Reprint. London: Longmans Green, 1952. A useful abridgment.

Preuss, Charles. *Exploring with Frémont: The Private Diaries of Charles Preuss, Cartographer for John C. Frémont on His First, Second, and Fourth Expeditions to the Far West*. Translated and edited by Erwin G. Gudde and Elisabeth K. Gudde. American Exploration and Travel Series 26. Norman: University of Oklahoma Press, 1958. Translated from the German original.

Ratcliff, Mildred. *Memorandas and Correspondence of Mildred Ratcliff*. Philadelphia: Friends Bookstore, 1890.

Schoolcraft, Henry R. *Journal of a Tour into the Interior of Missouri and Arkansas in 1818 and 1819*. Collection of Modern and Contemporary Voyages and Travels, 3d Series, vol. 4, no. 5. London: Sir R. Phillips, 1821. Reprint. *Schoolcraft in the Ozarks*. Edited by Hugh Park. Van Buren, Ark.: Argus Printers, 1955. Also contains Schoolcraft's poem "Transallegania or the Groans of Missouri, A Poem."

————. *Narrative Journal of Travels Through the NorthWestern Regions of the United States Extending from Detroit through the Great Chain of American Lakes to the Sources of the Mississippi River in the Year 1820*. Edited by Mentor L. Williams. East Lansing: Michigan State University Press, 1953.

————. *Scenes and Adventures in the Semi-Alpine Region of the Ozark Mountains*. Philadelphia: Lippincott, Grambo, 1853.

————. *Travels in the Central Portions of the Mississippi Valley*. New York: Collins & Hannay, 1825.

————. *Travels through the Northwest Regions of the United States*. Ann Arbor: University Microfilms, 1966. Reprint of the original *Narrative Journal of Travels*. Albany: E. & E. Hosford, 1821.

————. *A View of the Lead Mines of Missouri*. New York: Charles Wiley, 1819.

Seely, Catherine. *Memoirs of Catherine Seely and Deborah S. Roberts*. New York: D. Goodwin, 1843.

2. Other Materials

Alcott, A. Bronson. *Concord Days*. Boston: Roberts Brothers, 1872. An account of Alcott's life from April through September, 1869. In part a revision of diary material and written in diary form. The first pages discuss diary keeping.

———. *Conversations With Children on the Gospels.* 2 vols. Boston: James Munroe, 1836–37. Alcott's Socratic dialogues with his pupils, the publication of which resulted in the loss of his school.

———. *The Letters of A. Bronson Alcott.* Edited by Richard Herrnstadt. Ames: Iowa State University Press, 1969.

Dwight, Timothy. *Travels in New England and New York.* 4 vols. Cambridge: Belknap Press, 1969. This work was revised in epistolary form by the uncle of Margaret Van Horn Dwight Bell from his travel diary and other records.

Emerson, Ralph Waldo. *Nature.* In *The Collected Works of Ralph Waldo Emerson: Volume One, Nature, Addresses and Other Lectures.* Edited by Alfred R. Ferguson. Cambridge: Belknap Press, 1979.

———. "Self-Reliance." In *The Collected Works of Ralph Waldo Emerson: Volume Two, Essays First Series.* Edited by Alfred R. Ferguson and Jean Ferguson Carr. Cambridge: Belknap Press, 1979.

Hamilton, Dr. Alexander. *A Gentleman's Progress: The Itinerarium of Dr. Alexander Hamilton.* Edited by Carl Bridenbaugh. Chapel Hill: University of North Carolina Press, 1948.

Irving, Washington. *A Tour on the Prairies.* Edited by John Francis McDermott. Norman: University of Oklahoma Press, 1956.

La Hontan, Louis Armand, Baron de. *New Voyage to North America by the Baron De Lahontan.* Edited by Ruben Gold Thwaites. Chicago: A. C. McClurg & Co., 1905.

Morris, Governeur. *Diary and Letters of Governeur Morris.* Edited by Anne C. Morris. 2 vols. New York: Scribner's, 1888.

Parkman, Francis. *The Oregon Trail.* Edited by E. N. Feltskog. Madison: University of Wisconsin Press, 1969.

Schoolcraft, Henry R. *The Literary Voyager or Muzzeniegun.* Edited by Philip P. Mason. East Lansing: Michigan State University Press, 1962.

———. *Personal Memoirs of a Residence of Thirty Years with the Indian Tribes on the American Frontier.* Philadelphia: Lippincott, Grambo, 1851. Contains material about Schoolcraft's life after the years of the published diaries.

Thoreau, Henry David. *Walden.* Edited by J. Lyndon Shanley. Princeton: Princeton University Press, 1971.

SECONDARY SOURCES

1. Bibliographies

Arksey, Laura, Nancy Pries, and **Marcia Reed.** *American Diaries: An Annotated Bibliography of Published American Diaries and Journals Written from 1492 to 1844.* Vol. 1. Detroit: Gale Research, 1983. Additional volumes are in progress. When completed, this work will supersede Matthews's bibliography as the standard edition.

Matthews, William. *American Diaries: An Annotated Bibliography of American Diaries Written Prior to the year 1861.* Berkeley and Los Angeles: University of California Press, 1945. Long the standard bibliography.

————. *American Diaries in Manuscript 1580–1954. A Descriptive Bibliography.* Athens: University of Georgia Press, 1974. An invaluable bibliography, but far from complete.

Meyerson, Joe. Ed. *The Transcendentalists.* New York: The Modern Language Association of America, 1984. An excellent bibliography of editions, manuscripts, and other research materials of the American Transcendentalists.

2. Other Materials

Allen, John Logan. *Passage Through the Garden: Lewis and Clark and the Image of the American Northwest.* Urbana: University of Illinois Press, 1975.

Bedell, Madelon. *The Alcotts: Biography of A Family.* New York: Clarkson N. Potter, 1980.

Brinton, Howard H. *Quaker Journals: Varieties of Religious Experience Among Friends.* Wallingford, Pa: Pendle Hill Publications, 1972.

Callow, James. T. *Kindred Spirits: Knickerbocker Writers and Artists, 1807–1855.* Chapel Hill, University of North Carolina Press, 1967. A discussion of the relationship within a group which included a number of important diarists, among them Cole, Cooper, Dana, Dunlap, and Irving.

Dahlstrand, Frederick C. *Amos Bronson Alcott: An Intellectual Biography.* Rutherford, N.J.: Fairleigh Dickinson University Press, 1982.

Kagle, Steven E. *American Diary Literature 1607–1800.* Boston: Twayne Publishers, 1979. Twayne's United States Authors Series 342. A study of colonial American diaries, this work includes extensive material on the diary as literature.

————. "Introduction." *America: Exploration and Travel.* Edited by Steven E. Kagle. Bowling Green, Ohio: Popular Press, 1979, 3–7. Contains an examination of the relation between travel and exploration in American literature of the early nineteenth century.

Nevins, Allan. *Frémont, Pathmarker of the West.* New York, Longmans Green, 1955.

Noble, Louis Le Grand. *The Life and Works of Thomas Cole.* Edited by Elliot S. Vesell. Cambridge: Belknap Press, 1964. Vesell's edition of Noble's 1853 work still contains Noble's major manipulations of Cole's diary.

Shepard, Odell. *Pedlar's Progress.* Boston: Little Brown, 1937. Biography of Bronson Alcott.

Index